APPETITE
FOR SOCCER

JUMPING LEVELS IN THE GAME
...BY DESIGN

For Parents and Ambitious Soccer Players
12-16 Years of Age

TONY KEES

To You!

BOOK ORGANIZATION

PROPS

I owe much to all the former players who serendipitously entered my life and helped shape who I am as a person and coach. Same to all current players seeking excellence in soccer and life. Especially those who will use this book to take up arms and defeat lethargy and procrastination, and who will allow this resource to pull them into the future.

Thanks to Dr. Don Grossnickle, one of my great mentors in education who got me thinking about personal training and how human beings learn back in 1999.

Special thanks to Jonathan Spector, Jen Buczkowski, and Takumi and Sakae Ikeda for their contributions in interview form, and a nod to Natasha Konrad for editing, and to my good friend and rocker, Richie Hoffher (of the band 7th Heaven) for website development.

Also a big THANK YOU to the handful of friends and colleagues who test-read the manuscript and contributed with thoughts and suggestions.

And, finally, I dedicate this book to my late mom Deloris and to my dad Tony Sr., who together raised and supported and encouraged me in all of my sports and creative endeavors.

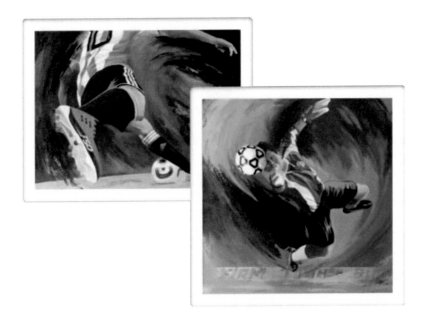

HOW TO USE THIS BOOK

Target Audience - This resource is intended for ambitious soccer players, boys and girls, field players and goalkeepers alike, roughly between the ages of 12-16. For the youngest players, the book should be read by child and parent or guardian. There are three good reasons for the parents to read the book: a) the parent can be there to help interpret the more complex passages for their child, b) the player / parent partnership is a key in getting the desired results from the book, and c) the parents will get a lot out the book as well, from the standpoint of gaining clarity in how youth soccer generally sets up! It will be part information, part inspiration, and part workbook.

For the older player, depending on maturity level, if you haven't already, it is time to take full ownership of your development and seriously consider the "add-ons" presented in this book.

Website Companion - This book is supported by a website that hosts the downloadable and printable worksheets that make up the workbook portion of the book. This content is key to the effectiveness of the step-by-step process presented here. Go to skilltimesoccer.com and click on the "Personal Development" section, then click on the "Appetite For Soccer" icon and locate the worksheet PDF file(s). You may want to do this right away and print all the sheets at one time and then use a hole punch and file them into a 3 ring binder (explained at the end of the introduction). The website is also a help hub where you can send in questions and reply to topical blogs.

There Is Work Involved! - There is quite a bit of journaling, logging, and graphing that is required to get the most out of this book, and it is one of the key components to its effectiveness. Just reading through the text won't do. If you want to jump levels and maximize your soccer gifts, you have to do a little more than you are doing now. Take heart. Below is just one cool example of a professional soccer player who started journaling when he was kid and continued all through his pro career.

Shunsuke Nakamura was a Japanese player who played with Celtic from 2005 - 2009. He was 30 years old when interviewed regarding journaling his technical and psychological side of the game.

He insisted: *'I am always honest with myself when I sit down in front of my soccer notebook. The words are an expression of how serious I am, so I cannot write with halfhearted feelings.*

'For example, the Champions League game against Manchester United in Glasgow when I was not even brought in as a substitute. Before the game, the manager explained to me the reasons why I was not in the starting line-up. He told me: "This game will develop in a way in which we cannot take advantage of your characteristics. I want to use taller players".

'Even if I was able to play in the following league game, I would not be able to enter the next game against a strong opponent such as Manchester United. Beyond that, I would not even understand what my weak points are and I may end up going downhill.

'I have to recognize and understand the fact there are certain areas in which I am lacking and write those points down and proceed to the next stage. If I don't do that, I would be wasting these great experiences that I am going through right now.

He continued: 'There is significance in applying pressure to myself by writing in my notebook. If I wrote that I needed improvement and then slacked off, that would be really uncool.'

Just thought you might like to see that the pros do this stuff, too!

Introduction - Part 1

My Responsibility To You

I feel two major responsibilities to you in writing this book.

1) **You get your money's worth** - if you're going to shell out your cash, you want to make sure you get full value.

2) **You get your time's worth** - most importantly, I hope you find that the time you spend reading this book and doing the exercises is well worth your while. Time is more valuable than money. You can always get more money, but unfortunately you can't get more time.

Here are a few more things that I hope you'll find while reading this book:

Sincerity - More than anything, I hope that you will find me to be sincere in my delivery. Sincerity is one of the keys to good communication. It's required on both sides. I already know that you are sincere because you are reading this right now! So I hope that you'll find me to be sincere as well. However, sincerity is not a test of truth. Don't make the mistake of saying, "He must be right, he's so sincere." Why? Because it's totally possible to be sincerely wrong! Having said that, this is not a book of right or wrong! There are just different levels of ambition and logistical scenarios that will directly influence the effectiveness of the advice and suggestions presented here.

Ideas & Inspiration - We can all use some good ideas. Good life ideas, good relationship ideas, good health ideas, good soccer ideas. So one of the objectives of this book is to share a whole bunch of good ideas that you can use right away. Ideas can be life changing. Sometimes all you need is one more in a series of good ideas. Kind of like rolling through the numbers on a combination lock. You might have 3 or 4 numbers, so you don't need a bunch more. All you may need is that one last number to unlock the door to walk through and discover a whole new you. Maybe this book can do that for you!

Also, I'm thinking that you probably don't need a complete overhaul of your game to reach your goals. It's probably more like adopting a few really good ideas or habits on top of what you already bring to the great soccer party!

You have this much going for you	You need this much more

I don't think it's like:

You have this much going for you	You need this much more

I'm sure it's more like:

Regarding "inspiration," that is a mystery. Who knows the mysteries of inspiration? Who knows why some get inspired and some don't? You were inspired to pick up this book and start reading it. Others were not (at least not yet). Inspiration - Some do, and some don't. Some go for it, and some don't. Some change, and some don't. Out of twenty, maybe five do, and fifteen don't. You are already in rare air!

This book was written for the believers. Those who believe in themselves - believe that they can change, make improvements in their routines and habits and reach their soccer and life goals. I am seeking you! I'm glad I've got a believer here today! You believed enough to pay for the book and part ways with your time and energy, and I appreciate that!

To get the most out of this book:

Be grateful - Be grateful for what you already have. If you are seeking upgrade and progressing through the various levels of soccer, one that you believe will catapult you to even greater heights, you must already have some quality about you. Be grateful that you can even dream about it. I think something great to remember is that you live in America, the land of opportunity (still). It has everything you need to be successful. All the books you need, all the information, schools and instruction you need, all the inspiration you need, all the challenge you need. Come on! It's there for everyone. You just need to unapologetically stretch forth your hand, reach for it and grab it!

Be careful, though, because it's easy to screw it all up by being cynical. This is the opposite of being thankful. Being cynical will shut doors and make you "less than." You would be sabotaging your journey if you are cynical about the people, cynical about the institution (US Soccer), cynical about the set up (your club), cynical about yourself, cynical about your chances. Being cynical just exudes a lousy attitude and It will prevent you from learning more, doing more and being more.

Listen Well - Rather, read well. There is some good stuff in here. Try not to miss it!

Do The Work - Be a good note taker, journaler, and logger! In other words, be a good student. If you make the work a habit, your benefits will go beyond soccer. I hope, 20 years from now you look me up and say, "You know all those exercises from your book? I still use those in my game (or my business)."

Take advice but not orders - This is a book of ideas. You might not be able to follow some of the steps for whatever reason. Just be sure that what you are doing is a product of your own thinking and contemplation.

Note: Before we get too far into the book, it might be helpful to know that even though this book was edited, the grammar and syntax were mostly left alone! That's because the person presenting these ideas to you is a soccer coach, not Shakespeare!

Introduction - Part 2

Operating On 6 of 8

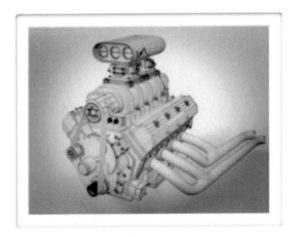

In addition to my responsibility to you, there are two main motivations for writing this book that you should know. The first is that after many years of getting into the hearts, minds and training habits of many talented players, it was evident that there were a lot of little things these players could've been doing that would've changed their game (and their lives) for the better. It was as if they were like a high performance vehicle with 8 cylinders in the engine, but they were only firing on 6 of the 8 cylinders! They were not optimizing. And this, my friends was the impetus for this book: *Individual Player Optimization (IPO).*

In fact, let me paint that picture for you. Let's say that you are a high performance machine that has 8 cylinders in the engine (meaning you are physically and mentally healthy, reasonably athletic and have supportive parents / or guardians). Chances are very good that you have been operating on only 6 cylinders every day! That's right! I'm telling you, after you get into this book you will see. It has to do with the fact that you are most likely doing what everyone else is doing: team practices, team games, a tournament or two, and maybe a camp. If that's the norm, would it not suggest that you should do more than that?

"Even if you are on the right track, you'll get run over if you just sit there"

– Will Rodgers

Things of value are on the high shelf. If you want to reach the things on the high shelf you've got to stand on the books you read, the games you watch, the advice you get from your parents, the wisdom whispered from a trusted coach, and your time on the ball. **These things add up to make a block to stand on that allows you to reach higher.** Don't settle for the things that are easily reached.

We will be looking at who you are in more detail than maybe you have ever thought before and what your priorities really are. Then we'll look at all the different things you can be doing daily to maximize your soccer gifts and be the best that you can be. Yes, it will be obvious that you can and should be doing more. You were meant to operate with all 8 cylinders firing, and the ideas and suggestions in this book are mostly about the last 2 cylinders that are not firing for you at the moment!

Which brings me to the other motivation for writing this book, and that is to help parents (and you older players) with the number one question that I field almost daily. That question is: "What else should my child be doing?" or "What else can I be doing." This is an important question because margins are getting smaller. The differences in training environments are not as drastic as they once were. There are many more quality coaches today than there were even 5 years ago. So if more players are being trained in generally the same way, how will you separate yourself from the pack?

Allow me to go off on a tangent here and circle back. In the U.S., sadly, sometimes the only metric some parents (and clubs!) understand is wins, losses, and scholarships. However, it is not that black and white folks; it can be messy and every player has his or her own pathway to get to where they need to go. It is not usually a smooth journey.

It doesn't help that many clubs can be reactionary in nature. They have evolved into businesses that react to what parents (read: customers) are demanding, and some parents may be lacking the experience and/ or resources to know what they should be realistically expecting. You want what's best for your kid, but your vision may be blurred and not congruent with the realities of elite youth sports, let alone high performance environments.

This book is meant to lay it out for you, as well as present a collection of ideas, creating a step-by-step process to make you a better player, fulfill your potential and increase the odds that you can jump levels in the game.

Introduction - Part 3

Making The Team & The 12 Steps

Everyone wants to make the team. Perhaps it's the Travel Team. Maybe it's the Academy or ECNL Team. The ODP team. The High School Team. The National Team. Making the team that you set out to make is an awesome feeling. Maybe it was a goal of yours to make that team. Sweet! Perhaps making that team meant that you jumped a level or two in terms of skill and competitiveness. You feel great because jumping levels shows proof of progress. The fact that you are reading this book means that there is a team in your near future that you would like to be on that represents a jump in levels of play, and you are seeking some advice and some ideas on how to make that happen. This book will deliver. It will show you how to systematically stack the deck in your favor and give you a better chance at playing your best soccer ever. I'll give you a heads up - you will need to develop an ability to focus on some targets and go for them, which probably means doing more than you're doing now! One of the goals of the book is to YANK YOU OUT OF NEUTRAL and PULL YOU INTO THE FUTURE! No worries. As long as you are coachable and honest in your work, it will happen.

Allow me to plant a seed. I'm guessing that you will consider yourself "successful" if you make the team and get to the next level of soccer. But, will that be the only way you define success? What if you work your socks off, and do everything in your power to reach your goal, but come up a bit short? Failure? Let me offer this: Later in life, in a results driven adult world, you may be in a situation where the result is the only measure of your success or failure. An example would be in professional soccer. In those environments, you produce or you're gone. There is no "Nice try." But for now, at your age the most important thing is the process. Stay true to the processes outlined in this book, work as hard as you can at them, and you will reap the benefits! Sowing and reaping. I believe a young soccer player is successful if they work at something they care about, put enormous amounts of intelligent, guided and honest effort into it, and at the end of the day, they say, "I couldn't have given any more." Even if you fall short of the goal, you will always be better for having gone through the process. That experience is yours, and it will help you reach your next target. Plus, you will have no regrets later because you at least found out how good you could get at soccer. Regrets later in life occur when we look back and wish we would have tried harder.

The processes presented here will be part information, part inspiration and part reflection. It will help you see clearly where your soccer fits into your life, and that information will help you determine where to direct your energy and maximize your soccer gifts. Everyone has gifts. Might be physical Speed. Might be intelligence. Might be a never-say-die sprit. Might be size. Might be silky skills. You most likely have a combination of gifts, creating what some call a "gift mix," which is a combination of the gifts that make up who you are. In order for you to maximize your gift-mix, you will need to explore your priorities. Those are the things that are most important to you right now. The things you care about most. The things you hold near and dear to your heart. As you go through this process, your priorities might change. We will take that as a positive! You are also going to find that this process is a big balancing act of those priorities. No worries. We got this! Together, we are going to dive into the following:

STEP 1   **Know Thyself** - Who are you, really? Bet you'll be surprised!

STEP 2   **Know Your Priorities** - You can't do everything at once. After you know what's important to you, then you need to prioritize.

STEP 3   **Know Your Surroundings** - How does everything work in soccer? Is it just games and practices?

STEP 4   **Own Your Development** - You will no doubt have some help along the way (coaches, parents, friends), but the degree to which you 'own' your development is totally on you and will be the biggest determining factor in how far you go in the game.

STEP 5   **Set Your Targets** - Setting goals and tracking progress.

STEP 6   **Get Smart** - Soccer Intelligence and uncanny instincts are a rare commodity in youth players, and thus presents an opportunity to make up ground on other players by working hardest on this area of your game.

STEP 7   **Develop Your Personality** - Explores a crucial but under-rated aspect of player development. Finding your voice and understanding your cause and effect on the game.

STEP 8   **Learn To Use Imagery** - The art of imagery and visualization is real and powerful. Use it to create the ultimate performance state of mind.

STEP 9   **Develop Your Personal Recovery Strategies** - Soccer is a game of mistakes. Learn how to let go and think "next play."

STEP 10   **Develop Good Soccer Habits** - Making just a few changes and adopting solid habits can make a huge difference in your performances.

STEP 11   **Ask The Questions** - This one is mostly for the parents of children up to age 14 or so, depending on maturity levels, etc. but the idea is to be brave and push the envelope a little and seek additional or enhanced training situations.

STEP 12   **Network** - This short chapter is also more for parents - there are myriad benefits to networking and is included here because it is important.

I think you will find this book to be like a personal trainer. It will be your guide through the peaks and valleys of competitive soccer. For this to work, you will need to be as honest as you've ever been in your life. It's going to ask you to go away and think. It is going to ask you to journal and log and write things down in charts and graphs. Stay with me on it. It's powerful stuff, and it will be worth it!

With this book, you're not on a trip. A trip is predictable and boring. You're on a journey, and a journey is full of discoveries and adventure!

So lace up your mental track shoes and run with me on this journey. Try to keep up; I run fast!

First up - let's get the picture! This part of the journey is like the pre-game warm up!

ASSIGNMENT #1 - **Get a 3 Ring Binder**

You will need to get a 1/2" thick 3 ring binder that has a clear plastic pocket for a paper cover insert. This will be your Soccer Workbook. Subject tabs are helpful but optional.

ASSIGNMENT #2 - **Make The Cover Page For Your Workbook**

Don't blow this off. Our workbook needs a cover. Let the artist in you shine through. I'm sure you haven't out grown it yet! I don't want to hear that you can't even draw a stick figure! In the digital age, with cut-and-paste technology (OK to have your parents or siblings to help you) there is no excuse not to be able to design a good-looking and meaningful cover page for your workbook. Use an 8"x11" piece of paper and fill it up with visual images that are meaningful to you and inspire you. Ideas like the logo of your current school or club team, and/or perhaps the logo of your favorite professional team, your jersey number, an inspirational quote or two, or a picture of one of your favorite players. Think about the colors. What fonts? Draw. Print. Cut. Glue. When you've finished your master-piece, slide it under the clear plastic on the front of your binder. This will become your go-to resource for making sure you keep moving forward in the game.

STEP 1

Know Thyself

"Today you are you, that is truer than true.
There is no one alive who is youer than you."

- Dr. Seuss

Alright, let's get to work. Do you know yourself? How well? Think it's not that important? There is a reason that this is the first step in your journey to maximize your potential as a player.

Look at the picture above and notice the kid on the left. Is that you? (Didn't think so but I just had to check!) Now look at the picture below.

Are you more like this kid? This player made a decision to do a little more, to go a little further than other kids his age. He is what we call a child prodigy, someone who is professionally trained and looked after in both team and private sessions. Athletes like this usually give up some of their childhood freedoms to find out how good they can be at something. Do you see the difference in the two pictures? These are pretty much the extremes at either end of the soccer development spectrum. So, have you ever thought about where you are on that scale? Are you shaded a little more toward the rec player or the prodigy? Somewhere in the middle? You will get a chance to draw the needle exactly where you think you are in one of the exercises coming up. By the way, just for the record, I'm not knocking that first picture. In fact, I absolutely adore it. I laugh every time I see it! It's real and shows kids playing soccer for fun. Nothing wrong with playing just for fun. After all, fun has got to be at the top of the list. Because if it's not fun, you will most likely drift away like so many other players. But it also depends on how you define "fun." I believe there are three kinds of fun: there is the ha ha, laughy-laughy, giggly kind of fun. Then there is the kind of fun that comes from when you win at something. And then there is the kind of fun that comes intrinsically, when you feel like you are improving and getter better at something. As a kid, I hope you experience all three...often!

"He who knows the enemy and himself will never in 100 battles be at risk. He who does not know the enemy but knows himself sometimes will win and sometimes lose. He who knows neither the enemy nor himself will be at risk in every battle."

– The Art Of War

So this chapter is about knowing thyself (yourself). In order for you to know thyself a little better, we are going to look at who you are, what your current ambition level is, and what your hopes and dreams are. We will also examine why you chose soccer!

What's cool about these exercises is that they force you to think about these things in detail and *write them down*! You will see that stuff starts to emerge from deep crevasses in your brain. Thoughts go from being hazy, fuzzy and shrouded in uncertainty, to crystal clear. When you dream, do you ever dream of being WORLD CLASS? What would that look like?Most players surprise themselves when they review their work. You may also be surprised!

"The thing always happens that you believe in; and the belief in a thing makes it happen"

– Frank Lloyd Wright

Learn who you are and what your game is. Biggest turnoff is being fake.

Instructions: Go to the website to access the work sheets. Print all of the worksheets and make as many sheets as you think you may need (you're only human - you may make mistakes and need to start over). Fill out all 3 worksheets as best you can and put them into your Soccer Workbook. Then, go over them with your parents / guardians and see where the conversation goes. It should lead to some healthy discussion and be valuable when it comes time to set some of your targets!

When you're done, I'll see you at Step 2.....Get to work!.................And have Fun!

WORKSHEET #1 - **The Ambition Scale** - a simple scale to see where you are in terms of your level of ambition and motivation in soccer.

WORKSHEET #2 - **The Dream Sheet** - a pretty involved exercise that requires thought, vision and a pretty good imagination.

STEP 2

Know Your Priorities

In this chapter we continue the work of knowing yourself even better. It is *important*. Remember, we are trying to "maximize", not "sort-of-ize." We need to be thorough in understanding who you really are and where your priorities lie.

Your life, your very existence most likely has these five components to it. What order would you put them in? Let's talk about each one in detail and then you can decide.

FAMILY - FAITH - SCHOOL - SOCIAL - SOCCER

Each of these components are separate, but each effects the other in some way. There will be some overlap. An example would be that your nutrition is directly related to your family situation and your parents / guardian's willingness to provide proper nutrition for you (unless you are providing for yourself, which I have seen for some players as young as 16). Another example would be your emphasis on school vs. your appetite for soccer. There is a ratio there that will effect outcomes for both. That's right. Too much soccer will take away from your school, and too much school will take away from your soccer. There is no way around that. There will inevitably be trade-offs and compromises. It's easy to say that it's a good idea to have balance in your life and not put all your eggs in one basket. But this might not be the best approach to reach any of your bigger goals.

In any case, this is definitely a family matter and should be discussed with your parents.

FAMILY - Your family situation is a variable in your soccer development, as long as you are living under your parents' roof. The level of support they give you is definitely a factor. There is a wide range of family dynamics out there, from 'Helicopter Parents' who tend to smother their children and are overly involved in every aspect of their soccer life, to "We're OK with you playing, but you have to pay your own way and arrange your own transportation." I have witnessed this range within one team. I have had at least a couple of players who had to get jobs to pay the club fees. This was interesting because they had a level of buy-in and commitment that most youth players never experience. Those players tended not to squander training time and never went through the motions in practice. You could tell that they were so grateful for the opportunity just be out there. I know that those players are much better for the experience. Would I recommend it? I will only say that it would be a cool experiment for a family who has the means to pay club fees, but consciously guides the child in acquiring a part-time job or chore to at least subsidize the fees, and, therefore, artificially create that sense of ownership and buy-in. This artificial hardship would, however, create a challenge in time management, with regards to school, soccer and social life. I don't know. Just a thought. But hopefully you are in a family environment that is loving, supportive, and gives you a balance of freedom and guidance. In some ways I am an amateur at family life because I haven't had a family of my own. But on the other hand, I have seen up close many different family environments, and the good news is that players have risen to the top from all different family dynamics, scenarios, and environments.

Something that I feel strongly about is a family vacation. Chances are good that if you are pursuing excellence in soccer, you have siblings that may be doing the same. Maybe not in soccer but perhaps some other endeavor of their choice. Which means your family will be stretched and find it difficult to find quality time together for any length of time. Having the 5:00 dinner together as a family is just about unheard of these days for the modern sporting family. Family is family. Time together is important.

That's why a family vacation can be so valuable. Not only for family bonding, but also for you to mentally recharge the battery. Whether you get away in July or August, which is a natural break in the American soccer calendar, or you have a winter getaway, it's important for your mental energy to be recharged.

Sometimes it's easy to not pick up on the fact that you are mentally tired because you love the game so much. If your family doesn't take a vacation, and you still feel like playing soccer, you would do well to at least take a break from intense training. For the hard core, maybe a week is enough. Maybe ten days or two weeks. Know thyself!

FAITH - Since faith is a life component for a high percentage of people on the planet, we need to add it our list of priorities to organize. The challenge for me is to not be preachy, only informative. So here is the best I've got: let's start with a definition. The word faith actually has a few definitions. One is that faith is basically a trust in what we can not see. Kind of like me having faith in you that you will do the work required in this book! But, the kind of faith that we're talking about here is more in a spiritual context. Faith in this context can be defined as *belief in a higher power not based on proof.* A lot of people believe in a higher power. According to an article in the Washington Times, 84% of the world has faith of some kind. "Worldwide, more than eight-in-ten people identify with a religious group," says a new comprehensive demographic study of more than 230 countries and territories conducted by the Pew Research Center's Forum on Religion & Public Life.

Allow me to give you a personal example that could help you in your soccer and life journey. The guy who wrote this book has been around the block a few times and has observed and experienced a lot of the good and bad in youth soccer. Even as a coach, you can sometimes feel mistreated and feel like 'life is not fair.' One time I was called into the office of an executive and he gave me the bad news, "We're not going to have you back next season." I looked him in the eye, smiled, and without hesitation said, "It's OK, in the end, we're all going to be where we're supposed to be." He was caught completely off guard by this and it disarmed him. We then enjoyed a nice 45 minute chat!

To believe in a comment like that takes a tremendous sense of self as well as a sense that there are things that you cannot control. You do the best you can, another human being judges you, and then it's another day!

Is the above something you can use when you feel down about getting cut, or not starting? I find the hard part in this is finding the balance between controlling the controllables and letting go of what you can't control (trust / faith).

So if you consider yourself *religious* or *spiritual* you will need to think about where this fits into your life priorities, so you can be clear about how it affects the other areas of your life, including your soccer. This is so individual and so private that I would not even offer a take away. All I know is that faith is likely a part of the equation in your soccer journey, and you will no doubt, at some point create your own sense of clarity on the matter.

SCHOOL - Obviously, school plays a big part in your life and directly effects your soccer. How? It effects your soccer because it takes up a big chunk of your 24 hour day (through the traditional school months). So there is an inherent equation here that requires you (and your family) to assess and determine the correct proportions of time devoted to both your soccer and your schooling. Let me share an entertaining observation by a coach that I have a lot of respect for. He was presenting at the National Soccer Coaches Association of America National Convention a number of years ago. His name is Tosh Farrel, a former Youth Academy coach for Everton, England. In front of a large bleacher full of coaches, he said, referring to the culture in the United States of putting a priority on education, "I think ya's got it right! I think ya's got it right! But, it hurts your football!" Boom! Summed it up in 17 words! Profound? At the time it certainly ignited a passionate conversation piece in my coaching circles. The more we learn about the cultures of the better soccer playing nations, the more we are finding that the elite players in the United States typically do not engage in their soccer as much as their counterparts. This is being addressed with increasingly more residential academies popping up, but so far that is serving a very few elite players. How many hours a week do you spend on your soccer? Let's speak in general terms. Let's say you have 3 practices a week, 90 minutes each. That's 4.5 hours. Plus 1 game. Assuming you play all 80 minutes, that's roughly 6 hours of soccer a week. Without too much analysis, you can tell you that this is not close to being adequate to maximizing any kind of potential. If this were to be your average investment, multiplied over a 12-13 year youth career, you would be creating your own artificial ceiling on your potential. So what do you do? Here is one idea that could help. Author's note: this is not for everyone:

HOME SCHOOLING - You know what is a growing trend? Home schooling! Could this be an option for you? Your parents should have a look at this. (CNSNews.com) - *"In the ten-year period from 2003 to 2012, the number of American children 5 through 17 years old who were being homeschooled by their parents climbed by 61.8 percent, according to newly released data from the U.S. Department of Education."* I find this interesting, especially since I have been coaching a number of home schooled players over the last little while. Personally, I feel that this can be a significant advantage for elite players. How so? Well, while those players are acquiring their requisite academics, they typically have more of their daily allotted 24 hours to spend on soccer. Simple math. Of course, there is more to it than that. Frequently asked questions about home schooling include, "Is there a significant tradeoff in ones social life?", and "What about the quality of the education?" This next part is more for your parents but it wouldn't hurt for you to read it, too. I offer this part strictly for informational purposes and in no way am I advocating for or against home schooling, as it is a highly individual and family matter. Also keep in mind that this is only one example and one testimony.

Takumi Ikeda is an elite '02 born player (U13 at the writing of this book) having been in the National Team pool and currently living in Wisconsin and playing for the Chicago Fire Academy in Chicago. His mother, Sakae, home schools him daily. Sakae has graciously offered the following:

How long has Takumi been in home school?

Sakae: He has been in home school almost for a year and a half. He is actually enrolled in an online school and there is a teacher for each subject. I act as what this school calls an "academic coach" who helps and makes sure of his progress.

What went into the decision to home school Takumi?

Sakae: In the 7th grade, he was starting to miss a lot of school days because of soccer related trips and activities, and it was getting harder for him to catch up with his school work. Also, the public school normally allows only 10 days of excused absences, which we had used up. We decided to try home schooling because it would allow him more flexibility in terms of the schedule. (Now that we travel from Madison, Wisconsin to Chicago daily for him to play at Chicago Fire, it is almost impossible for him to go to traditional school.)

Has there been a social tradeoff and did that go into the decision to home school Takumi?

Sakae: That was one concern we had when we were considering home schooling. Takumi actually contacted a few high school aged boys we know who are home schooled and asked them about it. They said they haven't had problem keeping in touch with friends who go to traditional school, which helped Takumi make the decision. Because of the amount of time he devotes to soccer, he was already not spending a lot of time with his school friends outside school and he would spend more time with his soccer teammates. So it seems to us that there has not been much trade-off after going into home school. He does enjoy interacting with teammates at Chicago Fire and spending some time with his local friends in his free time.

What would you say about the quality of education?

Sakae: We feel that the quality of education in this type of setting is largely dependent on how the student takes it and works on it and how a parent is involved. The quality of the curriculum is good. But it is based on reading the materials and working on assignments himself (and not the classroom setting), so unless the student is determined to seriously work on it, the quality easily declines. For Takumi, we feel it has been helpful in learning to be more responsible with his own progress since he cannot complete the courses unless he finishes all assignments given.

Additional Thoughts from Sakae:

When Takumi was in a traditional school, although he spent about seven hours a day there, I'm honestly not sure how much he was actually into studying and learning. Still, he was able to get by with pretty good grades. Now with this homeschool (online school) setting, he does not have to spend as much time but he needs to actually focus and get things done, and there are no other ways. And he is aware that he needs to get his school work done in order to keep playing soccer. I'm sure this is different from person to person (Takumi's older brother thrived in a traditional school setting), but for Takumi, I definitely see positives in terms of learning…I think this has also been a big part of "owning his soccer development."

For Takumi, how do use your extra hours in a day?

Takumi: I use these extra hours to train and prepare for training. I usually take naps to get enough rest between my trainings. Since it's a 3 hour drive to training each way, it's very convenient to do homeschooling for flexibility.

Do you ever miss being in a traditional school, and the social interactions that go along with it?

Takumi: Sometimes I miss the interaction of traditional school, but I have a goal that I'm aiming for and will try to do anything to make it.

Do you think your particular home schooling situation helps your soccer progress?

Takumi: I think it does. I need to think on my own and read each question carefully. I have more time for soccer and I've learned that if you have a good mentality when you study, you will have a good mentality while playing soccer.

So there you have an alternative view point from mother and son. Again, I'm not advocating on line schooling, nearly presenting an out-of-the-box way to potentially accelerate your development. My best advice is to evaluate the risk and reward factors as a family.

SOCIAL - What about this part of your life? Do you think having a good social life has anything to do with maximizing your soccer gift-mix? I'm going to say yes, because having friends and being able to talk about things other than soccer can actually help to energize you when you go back to your soccer.

Diversionary Tactics - It may not seem like it at times, but there IS more to life than soccer! Yes, I said it! If you have a love affair with soccer, and you get away from it for little chunks of time, you may feel stronger and more passionate about the game when you go back to it. But getting away from soccer by spending time with your friends is not the only reason to work at a good social life.

Support Group - Additionally, your friends, if they are true friends, can be a wonderful support group for you in your quest to be the best person and soccer player that you can be. You may want to share your goals with a select few who you know would love for you to succeed.

Life Skills - Hanging with friends and being in group settings can also be good for you because you will develop valuable life skills like cooperation: ("what are we gonna do tonight?"), conflict resolution: ("So-and-so is moving in on your girlfriend / boyfriend"), compassion: ("Sara is grounded, let's go cheer her up!"). Interestingly, most young athletes have different sets of friends. You have your club teammates. Then, if you are playing with your school team, you will have a whole different set of friends. Perhaps you have neighborhood friends, and school friends outside of sports. I believe this is healthy.

Feel Good - For me, one of the real benefits of having lots of friends is that you have a steady stream of people that you can make feel good! Not that you couldn't just go out and perform random acts of kindness for people you don't know, but friends are friends. The Golden Rule and being kind to people feels good! And, feeling good on a regular basis helps your soccer, because performance follows mind (read 'mood').

"The true measure of a man's life is how he makes others feel when he is with them!"

and,

"You can have anything you want in life if you just help enough other people get what they want in life!"

SOCCER - Ah yes! The game we love! What can we say about it? Somewhere along the line you decided that you like soccer. Maybe *love* is a better word for it. Can you verbalize the reasons? When you try to write about soccer, it seems to laugh and mock our best efforts to describe its beauty. But that shouldn't stop us! Our heart is captured by this game, but the heart is incapable of knowing anything about the strategies or tactics of soccer. The heart does, however know something about the human spirit which drives our efforts and allows us to experience the joys of our game. The game is the perfect playground for our free spirit to run, jump, slide, bump, fall and establish a relationship with the main attraction: the ball! There is something elementary and primal about the ball. Everybody wants it, but we know it must be shared, at least on our side! The ball itself is perfect. Symmetrical. It doesn't have an opinion and doesn't care about your team or the other team. And it is perfectly obedient to physics. It has no choice. Flying, curving, rising, dipping, spinning, bouncing, and rolling with complete disregard to your wishes, rather, only to the forces applied to it. I love that we can manipulate and influence those forces. In fact, we are 100% responsible for them. The ball just sits there otherwise. It is us who bring the ball to life. So is there such a thing as a lucky bounce?

Then, there is the shared goal with your teammates in trying to win the game, which is awesome in itself, but if we can feel that we are getting better at soccer, that is where the real intrinsic love for the game comes from (unless you're in an over 40 league or pub league of course! Then it's just like being 6 years old again and playing just because you like the freedom of running and chasing a ball). Don't laugh. This will be you someday, kid!

I also love that the game allows personalities to flourish. The person you are off the field comes into the game. Amazingly, the game also influences who you are off the field. It's perfect yin and yang. Your personality impacts the game and the game impacts who you are. You gotta respect that! If you play a lot of soccer, over time you will notice that how you handle the challenges in the game will shape your character in all matters of life. This is ultimately where the game has value.

As a young player you may not see this yet, and that is as it should be. At your age you should be playing freely (within your team structures, of course), and through the enjoyment of the game you will come back tomorrow and play once more!

We're going to take a little time out now to role up the sleeves and get busy. After reading the previous commentary on the 5 life components, you no doubt have thoughts of your own regarding each. There are 4 assignments to get after here so take your time. You don't have to do these all at once!

WORKSHEET #4 - **Life Priorities Assessment** After having read each of previous commentaries on Family - Faith - School - Social - Soccer, go to the "Life Priorities Assessment" worksheet and thoughtfully fill it out. When you are finished, do the "Life Priorities Rank" worksheet right away.

WORKSHEET #5 - Life Priorities Rank Simply rank, in order of priority the 5 components as you see them now. When you are finished, file it along with your Life Priorities Assessment Work sheet in your Soccer Workbook.

WORKSHEET #6 - Soldiers & Artists Scale A simple visual of where you feel you are in terms of being creative vs being tough and gritty.

WORKSHEET #7 - **Attribute Assessment** This is a more in-depth self evaluation of your thoughts about you as a player.

STEP 3

Know Your Surroundings

MYSTERIUM TREMENDUM! I love that term. I sometimes use it sarcastically in describing a player, parent, coach or ref who seems a bit, um, disoriented! (under my breath, of course!) In other, more recognizable terms - it's a jungle out there. What is soccer like in your area? How many different levels of soccer are there? Is it made up of the usual rec, travel and club soccer? What about elite club soccer, ECNL & US Developmental Academy, or the NPL, MDL, MRL, ENPL, AYSO United, or ODP and ID2 select teams? The bigger clubs will have professional, or at least licensed coaches. Other clubs will be parent and volunteer based. If you live in an area that has the 4 seasons, how about a variety of indoor and outdoor facilities in which to play? How many different indoor and outdoor leagues are there? What about Futsal? What are the differences in cost from club to club, compared to what they offer? How are the high school programs in your area? Is there a stable of local "professionals" that offer Private or Personal Training? How supportive is your local State Soccer Association? Do you know the difference between US Club and USYSA?

This can be overwhelming, so let me help organize some of the chaos for you.

I believe it's important to take a step back and look at how all of this is set up. It's really not a mystery. It all can be categorized which can give you a sense of clarity and understanding. Understanding is knowledge. Knowledge is power. And, power gives you a sense of control.

Earlier I mentioned that your soccer life sets up to be so much more than practices and games, so let's do a deeper dive and see what it reveals. I'm going to assume that you are on a *team* and have a regular schedule of games and practices. So let's start with *games*. The Game is a public display of what you have worked on all week. It's a performance in front of people, not unlike a concert, only the score is kept. Judgements are made and then we move on.

Performances are necessary as a means of measurement and progress, much like a test in school. The game, besides being fun to play, is what you are ultimately measured against. How good you are at processing game actions and solving soccer problems and contributing to the success of the team is how you will forever be judged as a soccer player.

These games, or *performances* are easily categorized. Some are league games. Some are tournament games. Some might be ID, showcase or tryout games, and some might be arranged *friendlies*. Each is a platform for you to perform. They all fit nicely into the category that we call "Performance Platforms."

LEAGUE MATCHES

This is the most common of all the performance platforms. Just about every player is on a team that plays in a league of some kind. There are some exceptions, where a group of players form a *Tournament Team* and just do tournaments every few weeks. But, most likely your team is in a weekly league, perhaps even more than one league. These matches are important for you. They are your opportunity to measure your performance against other performances and see if you are improving and moving in the right direction.

TOURNAMENTS

I think everyone agrees that tournaments are fun. The atmosphere at most tournaments is festive and is a celebration of our game. But tournaments, for me have always been more than a good time. I always noticed a jump in my players' performances in the weeks after a tournament. I believe there is something about multiple games played in a short span of time that assists in their development. It's kind of like *learn and repeat, learn and repeat, learn and repeat*. The lessons get reinforced because everything is condensed and intensified. Mind you, I don't think it is a good idea to play at 7:00 PM on Friday night, and then turn around and play a game at 9:00 AM Saturday morning. Most people these days are aware of the implications of a lack of recovery and so efforts are made to manage the physical loads of the players at some tournaments.

So, a balance of league games and a couple tournaments remains optimal in your development.

3v3 Tournaments? My opinion is that, although a bit gimmicky, it still has value.They are still enjoyable for the players and have developmental value as well. The amount of touches and the fact that a player cannot hide are positives.

TRYOUTS (ODP / id2 / College Showcase / Combines)

Though not official games, this platform still offers opportunity to perform and measure against the game as well as against other players. In this environment you are either trying to make a team or impress a coach for future consideration. There is a selection process and note-taking process. You have a short window to impress, so preparation is key. So is keeping your nerves in check.

Tip: Nervous is normal. Some players struggle with nerves going into try-outs. What always helped me in a tryout situation was self talk. After being nervous for a few days leading up to the tryout, try to relax and just go do what you do! It's a game. You're playing a game! You love games. And having the 'butterflies' is good - it's that state of readiness with a tinge of fear. Perfect!

FRIENDLIES

Depending on the match objectives, and perhaps with clarification from your coach, you could use a friendly game a number of ways. One way could be to approach the game with a mentality of being as error free as possible, seeking perfection. Another approach might be, because there is usually little on the line, to explore, experiment and express yourself at the risk of making more than your usual ration of mistakes. In other words, reduction of error vs. artistic freedom and expression. Perhaps you would be asked to play a different position, in which case it's the coach who is experimenting, possibly because a) he/she has been contemplating a better developmental fit for you or b) perhaps the move would be an experiment to see if it strengthens the team. In any case, friendlies should not be wasted as an opportunity to get better at *something!*

Practices and training. We mentioned just a little while ago about the driving force behind why we practice in the first place (getting better and winning). Let me tell you that the best of the best that I work with also develop another reason that drives their training, and that is that they have an intimate relationship with training itself. They just love to train. They develop an amazing appetite for training and work. Training becomes the game for them. These players don't take plays off in practice, and not only that, they don't take repetitions off! When training involves repetitive drills or exercises, each time they come up to the drill cue, it's game on! On their toes. Eyes wide open and focused. Body language sharp and ready. They are vocal, lively and bright. And the next rep, exactly the same thing! These type of players always seem to be maximizing. This needs to be you!

Let's now look at the different kinds of practice and training environments that are out there.

TEAM TRAINING

This is by far the most frequent of practice environments (for team sports). Team Training is efficient, economical and necessary to learn and grow in the game. After all, you can't play the game by yourself. But we have to be careful with team training sessions exactly because of their frequency and their one-size-fits-all nature. Typically you have 3-4 practices on the calendar each week, and it becomes easy to show up to practice just because it's on the calendar! There is a routine-ness that you must be aware of and work against. You cannot fall into the trap of showing up and just going through the motions. Leave that for for the ordinary players. Remember 6 of 8. Keep that in your head.

CAMPS

I'm a believer in camps. Especially residential camps. For you, it's a chance to live the dream. Soccer all day and night! Plus, there is the 'experience' and adventure of being away from home that creates lasting memories. I feel that camps are so beneficial, that there should be a way to structure yearly periodization to include a camp type of environment every 3 or 4 months. Day camps, which are essentially double or triple sessions can be awesome for a player, provided the training loads are not crazy. There is a reason that you see residency programs, high school, college and pro teams having 2-a-days! For me, the interesting thing about a camp is the potential for enhanced programming, such as classroom assignments, video analysis, advice on nutrition and rest, recovery and body mainte-nance. I believe a good camp is a fantastic way to make a quick impact and a noticeable jump in your game.

SELF TRAINING

This is one of the most important tips in the book. Self training is the mark of a player who is a seeker and self-starter, who has the ambition to get busy without parental or coach prompting. That is, a player who has the motivation, fire and passion to not wait for someone to tell them that it's time to train. These players are typically creative and use whatever spaces and equipment are available, like garages, basements, driveways and back yards. Tennis courts and parking lots. Open parks and anywhere that has a wall, like the side of a local school. Better yet, 4 walls, like a racquet-ball court. The things you can work on with just you, a ball, and a wall should not be underestimated. A wall is a non discriminatory training part-ner. It obeys the laws of physics and is perfect in its own touch and service. Perfect for working on your ball striking and touch.

But, make no mistake, Self Training is not just about bringing a bag of balls out to the park and practicing your free kick, or your moves, or your jug-gling record. Self training includes way more than this. It is about taking ownership of your development and requires you to become a "Deep Domain" expert and student of the game. This requires study. How? Reading is one way. What you are doing now is exactly what I'm talking about. You're sitting here reading this material and it definitely falls under the category of *self training*. Brilliant! Carry on!

Every time you read an article about soccer, or read a soccer book, or watch a soccer game on TV, it has a cumulative, add-on effect to your soccer development. It all adds up and counts toward your growth as a player. It's also a sign that you are striving and reaching. You are investing more than average players and you are "maximizing." Keep going!

Additionally, Self Training is a low cost, or no cost activity. Talk about Bang For Your Buck!

PERSONAL TRAINING

This is a big one. As of the writing of this book, the US Development Academy Program Philosophy states, in the first two bullet points:

★ Program is focussed on individual development of elite players within the team concept.

★ Emphasis on more training; and higher quality training

Pretty clear objectives that point in the direction of the individual player. This is music to my ears, of course because remember, this book is about *Individual Player Optimization*!

Unless your club is a residency program (where players are housed, schooled and trained together), odds are that your club is not a full-service organization (apologies to those clubs that may be), so it would behoove you to seek opportunity outside of the club to accelerate your learning velocity. It's not the club's fault. The economics of club soccer typically don't include you and one coach. Or, even you plus three or four teammates and one coach. At least not regularly. Unless, of course you are a goalkeeper in a club that employs a GK coach. And, this is where I think we need to take our cue. In my opinion, the goalkeepers and their coaches have it right. When I see a good GK coach working with six or eight GK's for 60 minutes out of a 90 minute team practice, I believe that I am witnessing the ultimate learning environment for the player. I also believe there is a way to do this for the field players in a team, and I know that some clubs are addressing this. Sometimes clubs have 'windows' in the calendar (periodization) where you can go outside of the club to get additional training. Still other clubs offer 'a la carte' training opportunities, with and without a fee.

In order to mimic what the GK's have going on, if you have the means, you would do well for yourself to investigate the possibility of seeing a *personal trainer* to attack certain parts of your game. Over the years I have had many conversations with colleagues, players, and parents about this and, through it all, my message has been consistent. Basically, a player's learning velocity is at its highest with regularly scheduled personal training sessions occurring simultaneously with *team training*. When I say *personal training* (PT), I'm talking about with a coach or trainer. There are variables, of course, such as the quality and personality of the trainer and what is actually being worked on, but, by and large, a player will improve quicker if he/she sees a qualified Personal Trainer once a week than if he/she doesn't. The reason is not so obvious. It's not just about quality repetitions and dialing in on specific training needs that are difficult to achieve in the one-size-fits-all team training environment. It's more about personal and individualized attention and feedback. In the absence of personal and direct feedback, efficient learning is impossible and improvement only minimal, even for highly motivated players.

A high percentage of high-level players that I've known over the years have gone to a personal trainer outside of his / her club at some point, especially goalkeepers. Sometimes with their club's blessing, and sometimes not. Unfortunately, your club or team coach may frown on you going outside of the club for instruction. The rub is always that the club can't control what is going into the player's head, and that the personal trainer may be reinforcing habits that the club would rather you not acquire. Seek personal training anyway. But, also seek the approval of your club, if possible. It's prudent and just good business. Remember, the player, club coach, personal trainer and the parent should all be partnering for the success of the player!

Unlike many of the team training environments, personnel training is a bit more conducive to a crucial training concept called "Deliberate' or 'Deep' Practice." In my vernacular, I call it *Technical Edge Training*. It's not what most of us think soccer practice is. It's way more intense, way more specific, way more focused and way more detailed than regular team training, and it usually only focuses on one aspect of performance, something mechanical and repeatable. Some of the common denominators are: *It's hard. It entails mind boggling repetition. The required concentration is so intense that it's mentally exhausting. And sometimes it is not fun.*

I believe that this add-on is needed for *Individual Player Optimization (IPO).*

Jonathan Spector on PT

Some of you may know the name Jonathan Spector. He came through the US Soccer ranks and signed for Manchester United at 17 years of age! I had him in ODP and then shortly after in personal and small group training. He has played at Charlton Athletic, West Ham United and currently with Birmingham in England. Jonathan has also been rostered with the US

Mens national Team as recently as 2015. This is an excerpt from what he remembers from those 1 on 1 and small group sessions:

What made you seek extra training in the first place?

Jonathan - I wanted to improve. Because these sessions were more personal, I felt that I was getting more attention and coaching specific to what I needed in terms of my technical game.

Why did you keep coming back to the sessions?

Jonathan - I felt that it was making a difference.

Was it ever tough to get in the car and make the trip for the 1 hour session?

Jonathan - Not for me! Because I was very active growing up playing a number of different sports and I loved every opportunity I had to play, especially soccer. I was in high school at the time and it was a sacrifice I decided to make to attend the sessions. My studies were never affected, but I did sacrifice time which I could have used for other things. Looking back it was a small sacrifice that I believe paid off. Through my experience of being a professional athlete, I've learned that in order to make it to the top level, and stay at the top level, you will be presented with choices and need to make sacrifices that will benefit your career.

Do you think you were the right age to start that kind of training?

Jonathan - I started with you when I was 13 or 14. It was a good time for me to start attending the sessions, but everyone is at a different stage in their progression in soccer mentally, physically, and technically, therefore everyone has to asses their own situation to determine what age is right for them. I grew up playing numerous sports including soccer, basketball, baseball, volleyball, and tennis for either a club team or in a league as well as running track and cross country for my school. When I started attending your sessions I was only playing basketball and soccer which is significant. It is significant because although I was still playing basketball, I felt that I could play soccer to a high level with the proper attitude, work ethic, training, and coaching which is why I sought extra coaching on a more personal level. I was beginning to specialize in soccer which is why the age of 13 or 14 was the right time for me, and because I had given up my previously mentioned after-school activities, my education did not suffer. Education was always stressed by my parents and from a young age that was ingrained in my mind and was very important to me. My parents were also willing to encourage and support my enthusiasm for the game which allowed me to attend these sessions.

Do you remember actually feeling yourself getting better and noticing it when you played in games during that time?

Jonathan - Because these sessions were based on personal performance, my technical ability clearly improved. It is not meant for tactical improvement which can only be achieved in a team setting. I also noticed an increase in confidence because I knew that I working harder than anyone else to improve. This increase in confidence improved my game as a whole. I learned to harness this confidence in my technical ability which made me a much more efficient player.

Looking back, what impact, if any did PT have on your development from both a psychological and a physical standpoint?

Jonathan - Psychologically I became more confident because of the repetition and (attempted) mastery. I greatly improved and my touch on the ball felt much more natural to me. Confidence and composure while playing are two key factors that allow players to reach their full potential. I also feel that PT had a positive impact on the physical aspect of my game, especially from the agility and speed work. The SAQ is important to any athlete's balance, agility, and speed which are major components of the modern game. SAQ is implemented in nearly every session at the professional level. We did this kind of work at Manchester United, Charlton Athletic, and West Ham United as well as with the US National Team. In speaking with professional athletes from other sports, it is evident that SAQ training makes up part of the daily routine for top athletes. Due to the repetition of practice, new skills became second nature to me which allowed me to focus my energy and concentration on improving various other parts of my game.

It should be pointed out that Jonathan played his club soccer at Schwaben AC and Sockers FC in Chicago, before moving onto the Youth National Teams and Man U.

Back to technical training and repetition. Some may think that soccer is too fluid of a game for such static and rote repetition. I disagree. For field players you have highly mechanical moments of skill in passing & receiving, shooting, dribbling. For goalkeepers you have shot stopping, footwork, handling crosses and rebound management, to name just a few. The goal of isolated technical training is to improve body organization and get to a place where you don't have to think about the mechanics; it becomes fast and automatic. This allows a player more free space in the brain in which to process other things like tactics and decision-making. I don't care what anybody else says, the laws of physiology tell us that you can improve and sharpen skill through isolated repetition. If the extent of your skill development comes from possession game activities, you are not maximizing. Your training is incomplete. You simply wouldn't get enough technical reps per minute to sharpen your skills adequately. I feel that there should be a balance of spending some time training away from the game, and then going back into the game and applying those skills under the pressure and flow of a game.

Jen Buczkowski on PT

Here is another interview with a professional player that I had the pleasure of working with when she was younger. Jen Buczkowski played her youth soccer for EG Arsenal & Sockers FC, then went on to play in USWN teams U14-U21, U19 World Cup, Notre Dame (National Champs - 2004), New Jersey Sky Blue (Champs 2009), Philadelphia Independence, Kansas City (NWSL Champs 2014 and 2015).

What made you seek extra training in the first place?

*Jen - I initially began extra training because I just loved playing. My team would have it's practices twice a week and on those other days, I found myself wanting to practice and get better. I remember going to the gym on a Friday night and participating in **Skilltime** sessions or going to the park in my neighborhood and using the wall to just kick the ball and work on my first touch and shooting. When I first started extra training I was only about 11 or 12. I didn't necessarily do it because I knew it would help me get a college scholarship or play professionally, I did it because I just loved the game and wanted to constantly be playing and having fun.*

The shooting wall across the street from Jen's
childhood home

Why did you keep coming back to the sessions?

Jen - Because they were fun. We always had music and the entire session was upbeat. The best part of it all was that a lot of the session was based on skills and me as a player. It wasn't a team focused practice, but a chance where I could get as many touches on the ball as possible.

Do you think you were the right age to start that kind of training?

Jen - I definitely think I was the right age to start training extra. It wasn't something my parents forced me to do, but something I wanted to do on my own. I enjoyed playing and had lots of friends that played. It wasn't extra work, but a fun opportunity to train and grow.

Do you remember actually feeling yourself getting better and noticing it when you played in games during that time?

Jen - When I first started training extra, I did it because I just wanted to play more soccer. I was pretty young and didn't recognize the value that would come from it later on. As I got a little older and more serious about playing competitively, I started to see a difference that it was making for me as a player. I could feel myself getting better and that translated to having more confidence in games. Practicing my skills and playing extra allowed me to feel comfortable on the ball under pressure and have a good first touch.

Looking back, what impact, if any, did PT have on your development from both a psychological and a physical standpoint?

Jen - Personal training didn't just help my soccer skills. The extra work I put in made me more confident as a player. I was able to understand the need for qualities like hard work and all the extra touches I did during the week left me feeling prepared for playing in games or big competitions. Psychologically, I knew the hard work and practice I put in each week and felt confident and comfortable to do anything I wanted on the ball. From a physical standpoint, I was always one of the fittest players. This was a result from all the extra training I did. When you train individually, you spend a lot of time on the ball. There isn't much time spent standing around passing with teammates. You are constantly working on your own and pushing your own physical limits. The more I did personal training, the more I realized how important it was to be physically fit. As a player, you can go through the motions or you can give it everything you have. With personal training, there was no option to rely on someone else. It's you, the ball and your desire to be the best.

You may or may not already train in small group settings or see a personal trainer, but, inevitably the next question you may have is: "What else do I need to know?"

What To Look For In A Personal Trainer

This can be difficult since there are different kinds of trainers out there, with different backgrounds and motivations. I know a handful of good ones. I also know, shall I say, an imposter or two! Additionally, I think it is wise to use a few different trainers, when possible. Though it is natural to gravitate to a trainer that you feel a connection with, try not to get overly attached to just one. Different voices and different methods can be good for a player.

Encounters with great teachers and coaches tend to be filled with feelings of respect, admiration and also a tinge of fear (of being pushed and not being let off the hook). They are genuine and sincere in caring about the player(s) in front of them, and they are not about the money. That's not to say that they are cheap. Good trainers should not be cheap. There is much value in expert, one on one, and small group guidance.

Good coaches come across as being solid, someone who you can trust and someone who is fit for your journey.

BEHOLD & BEWARE

BEHOLD the coach who watches you very intently. They want to figure you out.

BEHOLD the coach who doesn't talk a lot during sessions. They are very action-oriented.

BEHOLD the coach who is brutally honest and doesn't always tell you what you want to hear. "I'm not trying to make you feel better, I'm trying to make you BE better."

BEHOLD the coach who noticeably cares about you.

BEHOLD the coach who is clear and precise with training objectives.

BEHOLD the coach who loves to teach fundamentals.

BEHOLD the coach who outwardly loves what they are doing.

BEWARE the coach who tends to talk a lot and comes off as a know-it-all.

BEWARE the coach that seems to be about the money.

BEWARE the coach who makes it about them and where they've been and who've they trained.

After all the above has been given consideration, and all things being equal, go with the older person. Daniel Coyle, author of *The Talent Code* put it like this: "Teaching is like any other talent: It takes time to grow. That is why so many talent hotbeds are led by people in their 60s and 70s. Great teachers are first and foremost great learners, who improve their skills with each passing year. That's not to say there aren't any good teachers under 30 - there are. Nor is it to say every coach with gray hair is a genius - they are not. But, other things being equal, go with someone older."

OVERTRAINING?

There is much science coming to the fore on this topic. Though I am fascinated by it, I am not sure that it is as prevalent as some of the related articles out there would indicate. The science seems so compelling, but my eye and my experience are telling me something different. I have personally witnessed many hyper-motivated young and talented players (ages 12-15) who, by definition are and have been overtraining. By overtraining, for example, they see one or two different personal trainers each week, plus they have their 3-4 team practices, and then they play anywhere from 2-4 games a week, including futsal. On the surface that seems like a lot. Of course, there are many variables, such as the intensity and demands of the different training sessions. The point is that these players seemed more than just fine physically and mentally, often times dragging their parents out of the house to go to training! These players are on fire! I had many conversations with the parents about looking for signs of burn out, etc., and they were on it. They were aware of the potential dangers and were very sensitive to it. In fact, one mom told me that there was one particularly busy week where she thought it would be good to keep her 13 year old son home from a personal training session...and he cried. But, is it really too much? If you added everything up it would look something like: 4.5 hours of team practice and about 1.5 hours of game action a week (and that's assuming you play the whole game). Then 1 hour of PT. That equals 5.5 hours of practice and 1.5 of game action a week. That's 7 hours of actual soccer a week. Is that enough to reach lofty goals? I think the concern is less about total weekly load than it is about timing between sessions. Example: recently I had been meeting up with a handful of players from different clubs, ages 13-15, in a garage which was converted into a sports performance gym by the dad. I would meet these players there at 9:15 PM, twice a week, right after they finished their team training and we did about 40 minutes of SAQ and core strength training. Initially, I was concerned about the player's work load on those nights, but after a while, the players reported that they felt themselves getting quicker and stronger and practices seemed easier. Pretty soon word got out and we started to get 10-12 players each night, and could have had many more but we had to cap it because of space. It was a very cool thing to see. Then, the ones who live closest to the garage asked if I'd be willing to change to 6:00 AM sessions, before school! I liked the idea for a couple of reasons: a) spreading out the players team training and sports performance training was closer to optimal for physical development, and b) I knew that they would be sharper and more alert in the earlier classes at school. This plays into the whole argument about school starting too early and that teenagers are not physiologically cut out to cognitively perform well before 9:00 AM. Early morning physical activity before school, as reported to me by these players, seems to negate some of those negative mental effects! After school, a quick 30 minute power nap and some smart refueling and they are good to go again!

Imagine if you had a routine where you got up at 5:30 AM twice a week and did some sort of soccer workout before school. Talk about appetite for soccer! Besides, my grandma used to say, "There is magic in the morning hours!" Grandma's are not wrong!

SPORTS SPECIALIZATION

This is another area of concern for some. Early sport specialization refers to young athletes choosing just one sport to focus on, at the expense of experiencing other athletic environments. One line of thinking is that children will miss out on a well rounded childhood (one dimensional experience). Another is that young players, who do not experience the different requirements of movement from other sports will be deficient and lack a complete physical education in the long run. I think it is a matter of what age we are talking about. At eight years of age, yes, the above would be a concern. At twelve? Thirteen? I think there is a window between 12-14 years of age where those that aspire, those with big appetites and love of the game may think about specializing. This is a highly individual and family choice, with many factors at play. Years ago, when I ran my own club, which was a mid-to-high level travel club, we preached having a focus sport (soccer) and a hobby sport. Of course, times are different today, but the good news is that there are so many more clubs, and so many more options for players to seek like-minded players and families, and club philosophies that are potentially in line with your values.

The fact that kids are specializing at younger ages is a natural evolution. You could see this coming 30 years ago. Back then, players who did more got better than players who did less. Same today. Young players who spend lots of time with the ball are easy to pick out. But I am in agreement with some of the science out there that a young soccer player would benefit if they could find the time for a complimentary activity. When parents ask which activity would best compliment a soccer player, I say martial arts or dance. Both teach gross motor skill, balance, coordination, timing, discipline and focus, all of which are requirements of high level athletes. So do your homework on this, but please don't judge others for specializing or not specializing. Seek environments with like-minded folks and club attitudes.

Different strokes for different folks.

WRAPPING THIS SECTION UP

Playing the game is what it's all about! But, most of us would agree that at least part of the joy of playing soccer is getting better at it. Would you still play if you sucked at it? Statistics show that one of the main reasons that players drop out of soccer between ages 14 and 17 is that they felt like they weren't getting any better. This is going to sound a bit harsh, but, I'm sorry, if it meant that much to them, the players that say they left soccer because they weren't getting better at it should have set a better sail. I think it's simple: they just didn't have enough reasons to put more into the game, so they moved on. This is not a tragedy. It's just a kid knowing herself or himself and moving on. I actually give these people a lot of credit because sometimes it's not easy to walk away from something that you were doing since you were five years old!

Having said that, I would be remiss if I didn't give you a heads up, because I see this a lot for players approaching 16 and 17 years of age. Some players become conflicted because they are beginning to be more aware that they are not going to make the team, or get the scholarship, and are realizing that they are losing the desire that they once had. Not to mention that at this age, the usual 'distractions' come into play, such as cars, work and boyfriends / girlfriends. In other words, *life* happens! The conflict comes when they ponder how much they have invested in soccer and feel like they have failed themselves, and in some cases, like they have failed their parents. This is a tough life situation and, I cannot offer an easy answer.

"One of the hardest decisions you'll ever face in life is choosing whether to walk away or try harder."

– Ziad K. Abdelnour

However, I will go out on limb here and just say that walking away is not an option for you at this point. You are too young to fully know what you are capable of, especially if you have never tried any of the suggestions or exercises presented here. If you are near or aspire to be at an elite level, keep going!

STEP 4

Own Your Development

Own your development! The first thing that we have to agree on is that this whole thing is your idea. If you were pushed into this, put the book away and don't pick it up again until you are ready to own your development. The journey to maximize and be the best soccer player and person that you can be has to totally be on you. You have to own it. Yes, you will need a little help and guidance from this book and several people in your life, some of whom you may not have even met yet! But, the drive and follow-through has to come from you. You cannot be casual about this.

"Casual creates casualty!"

On Being Accountable

No one can hold you accountable. Someone may say "I'm holding you accountable," but that is a misuse of the word. What they are really saying is that you must comply, or there will be consequences. Compliance is not Accountability. Accountability is an expectation of account-giving, and comes from within. If you are accountable, you have no problem owning up to a mistake (part 1) and then seeking to amend your error (part 2).

Merely admitting a mistake without a sincere effort to amend or fix it is hallow. Both parts are necessary to be accountable.

You choose to be accountable—it can't be forced upon you. If you choose to be accountable, and this is definitely your personal choice—then be decisive about it. Accountability is ownership. Here are some ways you can "own" your actions:

- You choose to be accountable for your impact on others

- You choose to be accountable by being humble enough to admit mistakes in front of the group (account-giving)

- You choose to be accountable by producing maximum effort, always

- You choose to be accountable by making sure that your actions and behaviors are in line with desired outcomes

Commitment

I am going to guess that you are aware that setting out to be the best you can be at anything requires a darn big commitment. You are obviously committed at this moment. But, will you be committed five or six months from now? How about next year? Try this quote on for size:

Commitment is...

"Doing what you said you'd do, long after the mood you said it in has left you!"

Repeat that a few times. This has to be you!

Going through the pages of this book will be like a journey of self discovery that will make *what* you're doing crystal clear, *how* better to do it, and ultimately *why* you're doing it. If you don't know why you're doing something, any set back or disappointment will likely be a bigger deal than it should be, and it could turn into a show stopper for you. You can *do*, *be,* and *have* anything you want in your life, if you have enough reasons. When people fall short of getting what they say they want, it is usually because they just didn't have enough reasons. We will address this in the Goal Setting Assignment coming up a little later in the book.

Owning your development is a 'no excuse' policy. One of my favorite stories about this is one that Jim Rohn, a famous business philosopher used often. Try to imagine that you are setting out to go from point A to point B in a sleek sail boat, which represents where you are now, and reaching to your next goal. You may not know how to sail but logic tells you that sail boats rely on the wind for propulsion. So the wind is a factor in whether or not you get from point A to point B. But, what happens when the winds are not favorable? What happens when the winds change direction? What happens when winds die down? What happens when they become violent and create rough and dangerous seas? You get blown off course and end up at point C. Someone asks, "How come you didn't arrive at point B?". You say, "Well we had unfavorable winds and then the storm clouds gathered and blew us way off course." NO! There were other boats out there that made it to point B. Why? Because they trimmed a better sail. The same winds blew on all the boats!

Mr. Rohn insisted that it is the set of the sail that determines your destination. I concur. The set of your sail will be a bigger determining factor in where you end your competitive soccer playing career than whether you had favorable winds.

"When the wind is not blowing
in your favor, you need to be
skillful in the set of your sail!"

So setting your sail is about making decisions that change how you think or act. Let's just say that to reach your goal or goals, do you think you would need to practice more, about the same, or maybe less than you are now? If you were to give this some thought and decide not to make a change, that is still a decision. You decided to stay the course, to keep the sail as is. Was it the right decision? Time, of course would give you the answer, but this is where a little guidance and a little coaching may be helpful.

Remember this through the entirety of your soccer journey - It's all on you!

"If it is to be, it's up to me!"

STEP 5

Set Your Targets

"Life is like a game of soccer. You need goals. If there are no goals you can't win"

I have a confession to make. I never set goals as a kid. Doing the best I could at everything was automatic, so I didn't believe that I needed to set goals. I have since amended that error in judgement. The credit goes to my "Fit For Life" philosophy and my regular workouts. How so? One day I realized that I was actually setting mini goals every few minutes while working out, such as 'this many repetitions with this amount of resistance,' or 'in this amount of time.' If I was about to do, say 22 reps of something, that number is in my head as a target. I usually set my targets as 'Stretch Goals', where I know it will be tough to finish. Even though I have always felt that I could self-motivate in this situation, I always found that having that number was crucial, because often times I would be on rep 18 and thinking, 'that's it. I ain't got no more.' Without the number in my head, I would have stopped. But, because the number was etched in my head, I could not let myself down, and I would push through to reach the goal. The benefits of doing that are many. Such as learning that your body is capable of more than you think. Also, developing the habit of 'finishing what you set out to do.' And how about performing when you are uncomfortable (last 4 reps)?

It's a good idea to set goals. It keeps your eye on the ball, your eye on the prize. Sometimes that image is just enough to make sure that you finish, especially when things get a little tough.

The promise of the future is an awesome force. It is powerful. The promise of the future is the reason you get out of bed in the morning. The promise of the future is so powerful that it can help you overcome any adversity or setback...if you have enough reasons.

Reasons make the difference in how your life turns out. That and, of course, the set of your sail. Reasons make the difference in your appetite and zest for life and what you want from it. If you have enough reasons, you can do the most incredible things!

Listen to me, dreams and goals can become magnets. The higher the purpose, the more powerful the objective, the stronger the magnet that pulls you in its direction. If you have enough reasons, you can't help but reach your vision, your goals.

What's really cool is that not only do your powerful goals pull you in that direction, they see you through as well. They see you through the down days, the tough times. The days when you might say soccer sucks at the moment. Some people don't make it because their goal is not bright enough to see them through a dark day. Set your goals and make sure that they are bright and meaningful!

Goal Setting

"A goal should scare you a little, and excite you a lot!"

The deliberate setting of reachable goals and committing to the daily requirements that are necessary to reach those goals can be an excellent way to stay focused and on task. Some of the benefits include:

- Have more purpose and direction in soccer

- Make more informed decisions

- Be more organized and effective

- Be more enthusiastic and motivated

- Accomplish some uncommon goals

Pretty compelling list of benefits for setting goals. Those reasons alone make it worth the exercise of writing it all down and going for it. But, goal setting can be tricky because there is no guarantee that you will reach the goal. There is a fine line between belief and knowing that it is possible to fail. The question is, what would your response be if you didn't reach a goal that you set? Would you get all depressed and quit? Or, would you get out a new sheet of paper and make a new goal to go after?

There is an Argument Against Goal Setting

A paper from the Harvard Business School suggests that there can be side effects to specific goal setting, including a narrow focus that neglects non-goal areas, a rise in unethical behavior, distorted risk preferences, and reduced intrinsic (internal) motivation. They go on to say that goal setting should be carefully prescribed and monitored closely. Personally, I can see this side of the coin as well. By "carefully prescribed and monitored closely" they mean are you mentally tough enough to deal positively with working hard to achieve a stated goal and then not reach it? I will tell you that some will handle it well, some will handle it OK, and some will not deal with it very well.

Parents, what are your thoughts on this? If you are not sure, try working through a small goal with your child using the provided goal sheets. You can always abandon it if you are not comfortable with it.

Go Ahead And Set Your Goals, But If You Do...

"Is your day-to-day in line with your goal?"

So many young players tell me that they want to be 'D1' or pro, but then I see that their day-to-day effort is not in line with the goal. If you are going to commit to reaching certain goals, you must be conscious about your day-to-day. Always ask, "Is my day-to-day in line with my goal(s)?" You can't have a goal of playing at a top 25 college, or playing in the NWPSL or MLS or somewhere in Europe, if you don't work on your soccer in some way, daily. Three or four days a week won't cut it!

Character Counts!

Once upon a time I had a talented and driven player on a team that I was coaching. He was everything in a player that you could want. But, then something happened. He got a sniff of an opportunity that he really wanted and pretty much overnight changed into an almost unrecognizable version of himself. As his ambition went into overdrive, he was increasingly harder to work with. He became very temperamental and worst of all, lacked any compassion or caring for the people around him. His zeal blinded him so much that he was unaware of what he was becoming. You may have seen this, where someone doesn't care who they step on to get to where they want to go, as long as they get there.

Work hard. Be focussed. Be relentless. Be committed and driven, but ask good friends to keep you in check. Character counts!

Work hard. Be relentless, but ask good friends to keep you in check. Character counts!

"Be careful what you become while pursuing what you want"

Set your goals and track them daily or monthly. What would you like to accomplish at the end of the week? Month? If you reach a goal, reset it or switch to another goal. You can work on several goals at once.

WORKSHEET #8 - **Goal Setting Sheet** Follow the directions on the Goal Sheet for each goal that you would like to reach or achieve.

WORKSHEET #9 - **Goal Progress Graph** If you are going to make goals, it makes sense to chart and track your progress. Use the Weekly or Monthly Goal Graph to present a visual of your progress.

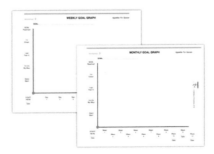

IMPORTANT - Have a sit-down with your parents to discuss your goals and how your family might support you in that endeavor. To get the ball rolling you need to have a conversation starter. Before you sit down with your parents and have this discussion, it would be a good idea to go in prepared. Have your Goal Sheets in hand and go over it with them point for point. Through the dialog you may find yourself adding, deleting and refining your Dream and Goal Sheets.

STEP 6

Get Smart

Soccer Player Tree of Attributes

"The best decisions aren't made with your mind, they're made with your instincts"

– Lionnel Messi

"Football is a game about feelings and intelligence"

– Jose Mourinho

This is an area that presents a huge opportunity for you. That's because so few players are smart in the game. If you can make steady progress in becoming more aware, more accurate and quicker in your decision-making, you will increase your value as a player. Playing on instinct, as Messi suggests in the quote above, is crucial. The trick is to develop your instincts and to trust them, but you can't trust your instincts if your decisions frequently lead to undesired outcomes (making the wrong pass, not organizing your body properly before receiving, arriving too late, etc.). Soccer instincts, and indeed, intelligence is such a commodity because it is elusive and hard to train. Some might say that this part of soccer is innate (born with), that some players just have that 'soccer gene.' When coaches in America get together and discuss this topic, it usually goes to 'culture', or lack there of as one reason our players seem behind their counterparts in other countries. It seems that American youth players can measure up to other youth players from the elite soccer playing world powers in both technical and physical terms, but where we fall down is in soccer awareness, nuance and savvy.

Notice the graphic on the title page. All soccer players should have a steady diet of the low-hanging fruit on the tree. This is typically the kind of work that Personal Trainers help with. To eat of the least consumed fruit, you would need to reach quite a bit higher. Remember from earlier in the book, "Things of value are on the high shelf"? Not that the low hanging fruit is not valuable, it's just the easiest to consume! Every ambitious player goes after the fruit on the low branches by seeking more training in those areas. The fruit at the top of the tree is not as easily reached or consumed, making it a commodity.

If you can chip away and make steady progress in your soccer IQ, you can really accelerate your development and stack the deck in your favor for jumping levels in the game.

Unfortunately, reading words on a page can only take you so far. What you really need to do is play every day and pay attention. Make sure you are totally absorbing everything that is going on. Watch more soccer. Read up. Study the game. I will do my best, in written word to give you some ideas that can help you become a smarter soccer player today. But first…

What Is Soccer Intelligence?

For me, it's a lot like speed. You can't teach speed. The best you can do is enhance it a bit, through cleaning up mechanics and improving strength and flexibility, and then learning how to anticipate outcomes and 'getting a jump' on plays (yes, mental speed). Soccer Intelligence is about an understanding, a knowing, and an ability to 'feel' the game. Knowing where to go, or not go, when to go, how to go, and what to do once you get there, which pass to make, which shot to take, whether to tackle or delay? For GK's, catching vs punching, coming off your line or staying home, choice of distribution? This is all part of an elaborate decision-making process that provides margins for making or not making plays, and margins that determine how good a player actually is.

Things You Can Try

Having said that, you can make immediate progress today by giving the following ideas a shot. Your team coach is probably harping on some of these things with you already, so forgive the redundancy. Note that the suggestions below are general enough to apply to both field players and goalkeepers.

Get ahead of the game - practice this by going into every training and game, telling yourself that you are responsible for your own awareness, that you will not rely on communication from teammates (as helpful as that is!), and that you will check over your shoulder often and never be surprised by players sneaking up on your blind side and nicking balls off you, and that you will take pictures and have ideas before the ball arrives.

Organize your body - shape up your body to make the next play easier by rotating your hips, body position open to the game, and usually sideways-on.

Pass to the safe side / lead them into the turn - pass to teammates in cooperative ways by playing to the side away from defenders, with proper weight, sometimes leading your teammate into their turn.

Move sharply off the ball - jump into pockets quickly and decisively, sideways-on and make good angles. Average players are lazy and casual about this. Being quick and sharp here buys time and makes you look more intelligent!

Read your opponents eyes - get out of the habit of staring at the ball. Try noticing your opponent's eyes as they process their next move. They will usually tip off their intensions and you can steal yards before they make their play! Other times, it may better to wait, so as to invite a certain pass before you and your team close in on them!

Predict outcomes / anticipation - practice moving early, anticipating likely outcomes, basing your decisions on visual cues (ex: in an arial dual between your teammate and an opponent, can you determine who has the advantage and can you move in the direction of where the ball will likely fall before contact is made?). How about spin on the ball? If the ball is spinning rapidly, which way will it bounce when it hits the turf? Be proactive, not reactionary. For center backs, it's obvious when the opponent will play over your line, so read serve and drop off early to avoid a horse race!

Make things difficult for your opponent - when you're on the ball, and you're seemingly out of options, can you come up with an action that makes the moment more difficult for your opponent(s)? An example would be when you feel like good possession is not likely with any of your options, so you lift the ball over your opponent's back line, making their defenders face their own goal, temporarily giving them a moment of discomfort.

Take mental notes of your opponent - you can get a pretty good idea about your direct opponent early in the game if you pay attention. Right foot or left? (you can tell by what foot they dribble with). Notice patterns of when they struggle. What don't they like? What are they good at? Do you feel like you are adapting your game to them, or they to you?

Playing conditions, weather, and pitch surfaces - take advantage of your warm up time to get a good feel for the playing conditions. Many games are played on synthetic turf these days, and not all turfs are created equal. Some play fast. Some play slower. Rain and wind are obvious factors, too. Don't let the game start and then learn about the pitch's characteristics on the fly. Games are 70, 80, or 90 minutes and you have no time to waist learning about something that could have been learned in warm up.

STEP 7

Develop Your Personality

When you think of things that make up a good soccer player, I bet you think of things like speed, skill, intelligence, determination, drive, and for GK's maybe things like technique, quickness, timing, angle play, shot stopping, etc. Those are all good attributes, no doubt. But I'm going to give you one more, and it's a big one for both field players and goalkeepers alike. PERSONALITY. In fact, it is so important that big clubs like Ajax have it right in their Player Identification Motto: T.I.P.S. Stands for "Technique," "Intelligence," Personality," and "speed."

Coaches love players with personality!

Find your voice and your way. If you are quiet, timid and shy, this is not a good sign. Being "quiet" is not bad in itself, but, it's the "timid" part that will be a problem later on. They say that the universe does not favor the timid. Certainly, high level soccer does not favor the timid, either. I believe this is right. Timidity will have to be worked on, and it can be.

The Quiet, Focused & Hardworking Type

Quietness, on the other hand can be a powerful form of personality. Some of the best players can ooze a quiet confidence, and they are focused, diligent and respected because their teammates and coaches notice, every single day, that they don't cheat. They don't cut corners and they never back down from a challenge. Additionally, they are relentless in their pursuit of their goals. This kind of player has leadership potential just based on example. To me, that is personality.

The Boisterous, Motivational Type

Then you have the talented and slightly more boisterous individual who always let's their feelings be known. They are the rah-rah players. They ask a lot of questions, tend to get on teammates in the heat of battle and can inject emotional, inspirational, and motivational energy into the team. This type of player also has leadership potential, often being able to keep the team laser focused, or a little looser, whichever is needed at a given moment.

Coaches love players with personality.

Additionally, personality is not all about voice. It's also about how you carry yourself. Things like your body language when you face tough breaks in a match. How you react to cheap shots, or even the manner in which you get up off the ground (or how long you stay down). It all counts. It's how you walk into a room with other people in it. Maybe it's how you defend a teammate or how you might resolve a team conflict. These all reflect personality.

But, no doubt, one of the best weapons that you could own is a well-timed sense of humor (I want to emphasize "well timed"). I read that sarcasm is a metric for potential. No lie. We can also reference **Oscar Wilde**, who once called sarcasm "the highest form of intelligence."

A little science to back this up: In an article in *The Huffington Post*, Jacqueline Howard wrote, "It turns out that being a sarcastic smart aleck not only requires social intelligence, but also may help you - and those around you - to be more creative, according to researchers." In the same article, Dr. Adam Galinsky, professor of business at Columbia University, said, "To perceive and correctly understand sarcasm we have to recognize there is a difference between the stated and the intended meaning. One of the main benefits that we know of is creativity and this flexibility of thought."

In high performance environments where everyone is talented, many coaches seek personality in players for potential. Coaches love players who ooze personality, one way or the other!

STEP 8

Learn To Use Imagery

Older players and pros know about this. This is not *hocus pocus* or *abra kadabra* and *alakazam!* This stuff works and it is powerful.

Research shows that it is possible to improve sports performance by using specific mental skills and techniques, including imagery and self-hypnosis.

What is imagery? Imagery, sometimes called visualization, mental rehearsal or self-hypnosis, refers to specific techniques often used by psychologists to help individuals visualize or mentally rehearse a desired event.

It involves using all of the senses to create an imagined experience that feels real. When you close your eyes and get deep into this, your brain is not capable of determining if the experience was real or imagined. If you do enough of this, you can pre-program the muscle contractions and breathing required to execute plays of your designing. How cool is that? You get to design the outcomes of your upcoming performance, and your brain can't tell if it's real or imagined!

Doing Within When You're Doing Without

Another cool benefit of imagery is that if you do this enough, your brain stores it up and counts it as *experience*. So, depending on how often you do it, and how vivid and detailed you make the images, you can be gaining valuable experience even when you are not on the field. This is called "Doing within when you're doing without." If you can't be on the field, you do the next best thing!

There are famous stories out there giving accounts that seem unreal. One is of a prisoner of war who, locked in his cell for years on end, fought off boredom by playing imaginary rounds of golf in his head. After he was released, with only a couple of weeks of practice he competed at a high level on the golf tour!

This is proven to work. It is backed by science and is used by the highest level athletes on the planet.

How to Use Imagery: 5-10 minute session

When? It makes good sense to practice imagery in the same way you would hydrate for a match. Hydration begins days before the competition. So should imagery.

1. Sit in a comfortable place where you won't be interrupted. You can even lay down with your feet up on a chair or bench.

2. Relax your body and take several long, slow breaths.

3. Close your eyes and begin to create a vivid and convincing image of yourself performing at a high level.

4. Get into detail. Imagine the sights (opponent's uniform color), sounds (player chatter, both teams), tastes (sports drink), feelings (exited) and even smells (fresh cut grass) of the experience. Raining? Windy? Sunny? Night game?

5. Picture yourself executing and making all the plays that are usually required of you.

6. Replay certain plays of your choice for emphasis.

7. Throw in some soft mistakes and picture yourself recovering from them.

Loss Of Focus

If the session goes bad, either from a distraction or simply that your mind is wandering, and you can't stay focused, let it go, Try to get back into the game, kind of like a recovery technique for imagery!

If that doesn't work, try a complete reset. Open your eyes, get up, and move a bit. Notice your breathing ,and when you're ready, try again.

Music

Music, like faith is so personal that it is almost pointless to make recommendations about it. But, allow me to touch on this because music can be a factor in your performance. There is a difference, though between listening to music while you are training to when you are using imagery or meditating. Listening to music while you train or workout is proven to enhance performance by as much as 10% (arousal and muscular contractions). When you're training on your own, this can be beneficial. As for imagery and meditation, perhaps something other than your favorite music would be helpful. Something not so familiar, because it is not likely that you'll hear your favorite songs during a match. So maybe something dreamy or mellow to take you away. Play around with this. It can give you an edge.

STEP 9

Develop Your Personal Recovery Strategies ('Next Play')

"We can't change what happened, but we can change what happens next."

I want to qualify the information in this chapter by saying that this falls under Sports Psychology, which, by nature is highly individual. However, I am going to use a broad brush in painting this picture for you because a) I believe this applies to most athletes, and b) this is not necessarily a sports psychology book that psycho-analyzes personalities and then develops coping strategies.

I feel that designing personal recovery strategies is important enough to make it one of the steps in the process of jumping levels in soccer. How you deal with setbacks can make or break you in high performance environments.

Mistakes happen. So much so that it's a bit ironic that we call soccer "the beautiful game." Yes, sometimes the play on the field fits the description.

But mostly it doesn't. Look at the game closely and you will notice that soccer is a game of mistakes. It really is a game of turnovers. Such is the nature of all "transition" sports, like hockey, basketball, lacrosse, team handball, etc. Each turnover represents a mistake of some kind by the attacking player(s). Over the course of a full match, that's a lot of mistakes. You know all of the common mistakes. Bad touch. Bad pass. Bad shot. Bad hands (GK). Anything too slow. Some mistakes are deemed worse than others.

One way to categorize mistakes is like this:

Soft Mistakes are the on-going turnovers that occur all over the field but don't immediately affect the scoreboard. They don't seem harmful in nature but, depending on their frequency can definitely impact momentum.

Hard Mistakes are the ones that are glaring blunders that either create crisis for your team while defending (ex: missed assignment leads to goal conceded) or on the other end you squander a golden scoring opportunity. These kinds of mistakes immediately impact the scoreboard.

Regardless of the type of mistake(s) that you commit, it is important to have a strategy to let go and move on rather quickly.

Your goal here is to work at developing a "next play" mentality.

Good players are both accountable for when they make mistakes and also able to let go and move on. They acknowledge the mistake, but they don't dwell on it. The ability to do this is important and achievable for every player.

Recovering From Mistakes

Many elite performers in all sports have developed their own strategies to get them back on track when they are experiencing a rough patch in a game or have made a pretty costly mistake for their team. Usually, the strategy involves self-talk, a very quick reciting of words from a check list that they either developed on their own, or possibly with the help of their coach or sports psychologist. The example below shows a simple, three-liner. This player uses a color as a trigger to redirect the brain and get back to "center." Then an action item. Then a readiness statement.

1. "Stay in the **GREEN**"

2. "Breath"

3. "Next play"

Try making your own recovery strategy list. Maybe it will be one word. Maybe only two lines. Whatever. It's personal, but remember why you're doing this. It is intended as a recovery exercise for when you are struggling in practices or games.

In Germany there is a word -"Nervenstärke" (pronounced "NAIR-fun-SHTERK-uh") that translates as "nerve strength," which is more than just a solid trait for a soccer player, but also a kind of living force in which German players have a lifelong relationship.

Manuel Neuer, Germany's top mens goalkeeper and one of the best in the world at the moment, describes it like this: "Since I was a little boy and started playing in the goal, my coaches told me about it and what it means for a goalie," he says. "It is a mental thing, where at every moment, no matter what, you are starting at zero. You stay calm. You don't dwell on mistakes." This applies to all soccer players, not just goalkeepers. "Nerve Strength" needs to be a characteristic of yours. All elite performers, in all sports have this in some way.

Another strategy is...**Smile**! A smile disarms the negativity that comes from a mistake. And a little science for you - enjoyment comes before achievement, not the other way around. Have you ever tried smiling (or even laughing) during a 'big' game? Smiling and laughing produce endorphins, which are strong mood enhancers. Not to say you should be all laughy and giggly, but a mature smile or even a wink to a teammate in pressure situations can go a long way in keeping yourself and your teammates from getting overly uptight and sabotaging performance.

"Failure is not fatal"

A good strategy going into any practice or game is to accept the fact that you are going to make a handful of mistakes. So don't sweat it. But also, don't take a casual approach either. Remember, *casual creates casualty*. Find your balance.

Recovering From Tough Losses

Case Study: As a kid, I was one of the worst losers imaginable. I felt embarrassed to lose at anything and I had various reactions to losing. I even had similar reactions when my beloved Blackhawks (hockey) lost! Couldn't handle it. I was a little baby about it. When I experienced losing, whether in organized sports or the play ground, I had a range of reactions, from pouting, to making a scene, to seeking solitary confinement, like under my bed or in my closet! I'm telling you, it wasn't pretty! But...

When I started coaching I was immediately thrown into the role of framing my players' experience's and counseling them in the ways of post game etiquette and behavior. I, as a leader, was myself learning the graces of sportsmanship, respect and honor, etc. Since by then I knew that my post game behaviors as a kid were not admirable, and coupled with my belief in practicing what I preached, I had to begin the process of change. And change, I did. I learned that being outwardly gracious after a loss, even a tough loss, did not change how I felt about the game. After the pleasantries, I could go home and behave any way I wanted. But while I was still at the field, I had to show respect, no matter what.

Not only did I learn the graces, but I got good at them. And, if any of the above sounds familiar, so should you. Developing a good reputation as a fierce competitor and respectful teammate (or opponent) goes a long way for a player...like getting invited to 'stuff'!

But, Houston, we (may) have a problem! And the problem, to my way of thinking, is the opposite of the above, and way too prevalent these days for competitive coaches such as myself! For me it is worse when a player is outwardly indifferent about losing a competitive game. I hope this is not you. I hope that you feel somewhat gutted after a tough loss, because this means that you cared more and most assuredly gave more than the player who can let it go so easily. Of course, I have to qualify this statement based on how much a player played. Let's be real; if you only played 10-15 minutes, that would be different than if you played all 80 minutes because the level of fatigue and investment is not the same. I'm talking about the ones who play 80 minutes and seemingly play hard for the team, but then are laughing and playing grab-ass 15 minutes after a gut wrenching loss. You probably have or had teammates like this. Maddening for those of us that care. If that's in you, you won't get to where you want to go in the game, and probably in life, either. Don't ever be that guy / gal while you are playing competitively and trying to reach goals.

It boils down to this: the level of disappointment and heartache is proportionate to the level of investment, whether it's one game or a season. When you pour your heart and soul into something and it doesn't go your way, that's when it gets tough. It hurts, as it should. But, how you deal with it will add to your growth as a player and person.

The Toughest Of All Losses

In my experience, by far the toughest losses that I have been a part of have been the ones that end a high school varsity season. I'm sure ditto for college seniors. In very general terms, the high school season is short, but intensive. Six days a week for two and a half to three months. Close bonds are forged and intense memories are made, and when it finally ends, there will be tears, except for one team. The finality for the seniors hits hard. If you get to this point in your future, the best I've got is this: let it hurt, but…

> "Don't be sad that the season ended, be glad that the season happened"

This is little consolation, but after you recover you will see the wisdom in it.

So after all of this, I'll share two more quotes that I used often early on in my coaching career:

> "There is no shame in losing. The only shame occurs when one doesn't care if they've won or lost"

> and...

> "Losing should ruin your day, but not your life"

Competitiveness is essential for jumping levels in the game. You can only go so far without a competitive desire.

Now take the Soccer Situation Survey. This will help you think about a variety of soccer situations where a positive response is necessary. What are your thoughts about how the ideal player responds?

WORKSHEET #10 - The Ideal Response Sheet Lists some scenarios a soccer player may face at different times in a season and thinking about, and creating the ideal player response.

STEP 10

Develop Good Soccer Habits

Work On Yourself As Much As You Work On Your Game

FAILURE: A few errors in judgement repeated everyday will accumulate and sabotage your efforts.

SUCCESS: A few simple disciplines, practiced everyday will have you on your way to maximizing your potential and reaching your goals.

This Chapter emphasizes the need to go to work on yourself as much as on your soccer. Eliminate the errors in judgement and replace them with some of the disciplines shown here. You will never be the same!

IT ALL STARTS WITH ATTITUDE

Many players have no idea how important their body language is. It's the first indicator that there is something psychological going on with the player. Most teachers and coaches are body language experts, and players will unconsciously sabotage their stock in a coach's eye with poor body language. Of course, it all starts with attitude. If you have a great attitude going into a practice or game, it would be impossible to have bad body language. The same is true the other way around. If you have a poor attitude, for example, pouty and sulky, your shoulders will droop and you will project indifference, looking like you don't care. The reason is simple. The body always follows the mind. You gotta have a good mindset between the ears first. The body will follow. That is a fact of sports psychology. That is why self-talk and visualization techniques really work.

Having said that, you are human. Sometimes, you're just not feeling it on a given day (hopefully those are rare). A good strategy would be to imagine somebody important is watching you at all times. Someone like a scout from a college or professional team, coming just to observe you and to see if you might have the right stuff. Imagine that this person has eyes on you in between activities. I'm talking about how you come off the field and how you go back onto the field. I'm talking about where your eyes are when the coach is talking. This stuff adds up, positively or negatively, and it's an easy fix to push this one into the asset column, especially when you remember what your mission is. Yes, this is a mind game you play with yourself, but it works and keeps you on your toes.

EVERYDAY HABITS

The list below shows simple habits and not really extraordinary but help make up the whole person and put you in the asset column of life every day. These are not likely to separate you from other players on the field, but they can go a long way when noticed by coaches who have to make tough decisions on whether or not you make their team. Besides tipping the scale in your favor, when you can check off most or all of these habits you start to become a person of value that other people will want to spend more time with. Consider these as a minimum standard.

1. **Preparation** - Get in the habit of checking your bag and making sure you have everything you need for practice and games. It's not your parents' job! Take ownership of this.

2. **Punctuality** - Be punctual. As a young player I know this is out of your control, but hopefully you and your parents can arrange at least one or two practices a week where you arrive early and can perhaps stay late to work on a part of your game.

3. **Dress Code** - Look the part. If your team doesn't have a training kit (dress code for practice), at least look like a soccer player (no basketball shorts). Look good, feel good, play good!

4. **Eye Contact** - Always make eye contact with your coaches and trainers as you arrive, during instruction, and before you leave. Be totally present and committed. No blank stares or wandering eyes.

5. **Helpful** - Go out of your way to be helpful, asking coach if he or she needs help setting up or cleaning up after practice and games.

DIFFERENTIATORS

The next set of habits are the ones that make the biggest impact on performance. These are non-negotiable and need to be adopted by you now.

1. **Objectives** - Know what YOUR training objectives are in case the team objectives are not stated. Make yourself a cheat-sheet based on your stated goals and review before practice. Things like "check shoulder often", and "limit unforced errors", and "have perfect distribution" (GK's), and "be more aggressive."

2. **Work Ethic** - Take no reps or plays off. Always be tuned in and turned on. Working hard has to become a habit, not a sometimes

thing. It needs to be a normal, everyday expectation of yourself, on and off the field.

3. **Honorable** - Honor the game by always going hard against your teammates in practice. You do them no favors by going easy on them. Honor them by making life difficult for them. It makes everyone better. 'As iron sharpens iron, so man sharpens man.'

4. **Nutrition** - Eat and hydrate properly, and time your intake. Proper nutrition is necessary and, of course, needs to become a habit. Like punctuality, this is a shared habit with your parents. Your body is a perfect machine that responds to your lifestyle choices. Clean up your eating habits, and you'll be amazed by the results.

5. **Sleep** - Get enough sleep. If you don't get 9-10 hours, make up for it with a nap. Daily rest is very underrated as a performance enhancer.

6. **Watch** - Get in the habit of watching as much soccer as you can. Of course, watch games, but Youtube and Vimeo are great sources to locate compilation videos that can both educate and inspire you.

7. **Read** - See if you can begin to find and read articles and books on soccer, as well as sports performance and psychology. There are many out there, but a good start would be US Youth Soccer's "Fuel" magazine. usyouthsoccer.org

8. **Solo Practice** - Learn to train solo with and without the ball, when no one else is watching. No external judgement. Complete freedom.

9. **Journaling** - Develop the discipline and routines of reflecting about your performances in your journals and logs. Develop the ability to not over-analyze, but rather give thoughtful, honest consideration to performances and evaluations.

Speaking of journaling, here is your next assignment. This is a detailed daily performance log where you rate your practice and match performances with a number from 1-10 (10 being the best you have ever played), and also log when you read an article or book or watch a game. See if you can detect patterns of good or bad form, on what days and where in the calendar year. Maybe there are reasons for dips in form or a spike in energy and performance. It would be helpful to see an overview of your performances to help you strategize how you might make changes and if your rituals, routines ,and regimens need adjusting.

WORKSHEET #11 - **Performance Log & Criteria Sheets** Keep track of and rate your weekly practices and games based on the criteria sheets.

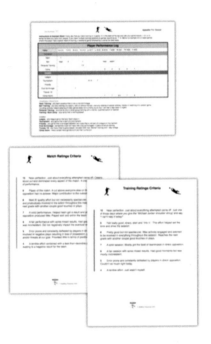

STEP 11

Ask The Questions

Getting ahead, reaching your goals, maximizing your gifts, and satisfying your appetite for soccer means not compromising. Your club may only offer so much. Stand up and shout! Take the initiative. Good coaches like when their players are engaged like that. Don't worry. If you use good tact and are sincere, then no caring coach is going to resent you for asking these thoughtful questions of them. Unless...unless either of you (player or parent) has an air of entitlement about you. Then you can expect a push-back. Coaches talk amongst themselves often about the 'entitlement factor' and they don't like it!

"The hard part, of course, will be not mixing up your signals about taking the initiative with coming across as seeming entitled."

If coaches seem irritated by the question(s), then either they were caught off guard and are most likely threatened by questions they don't feel they can answer, or possibly the questions didn't roll off your tongue the way you wanted them to, in which case you would need to rephrase.

Whether you are a member of a pay-to-play model club or a fully funded club, you are still owed this much.

Get an evaluation from coach - By now you should know quite a bit about yourself, but it would be helpful if you knew how your coach felt about you. If you are not expecting an evaluation from your coach, make it a priority to politely ask for one. Preferably a written one. If it is not your club's policy to do this, then at least ask for a verbal review. Most clubs do this much. You will just need a good memory so when you get home you can jot down your coach's general thoughts about you. It is important to know where you stand in your coach's eyes. You can use an evaluation as something to measure against. Then put it in your workbook.

Ask coach if you can train "up" - If you feel that you are one of the better players on your current team, you owe it to yourself to explore this option. Interestingly, US Soccer conducted a survey of American National Team and professional players, asking them to rank in order, the scenarios that they felt contributed most to their advancement in the game. The number one factor, according to the players, was playing up! Usually, this arrange-ment allows you to continue to train and play with your current team and also be stretched once or twice a week with an older team in your club. It is not uncommon among true developmental clubs to have arrangements like this. Sometimes it's called pool training, where players grouped by certain criteria. It's tricky though! If your club has a history of moving play-ers up, don't ask. They have already thought about it. If your club does not have a history of moving players up, at least for training, then pick your spot and use good tact in broaching the subject. Beware, though. Ask this question with caution. This question expressed in the wrong way could be interpreted as being presumptuous. You have to know if the coach is approachable or not and read the situation. You don't want to be put in bad standing with the coach or club. Best to bring it up either toward the end of a good conversation with your coach, perhaps during a review or evaluation, or upon joining a new club. Some clubs will not promote the better players (vertical Integration) because it can potentially weaken their teams up and down the ranks. I want to reiterate and emphasize that you should not be asking about this if you are not one of the better players on your team.

Something else you might try, however, is to jump on a Futsal team with older players. A player with a big appetite for soccer and desire to improve can hang out all day at either of my Futsal facilities and can usually get in on 2-4 games. We call these players "gym rats." Don't worry, that is a good term and considered a compliment. Be a gym rat!

Ask coach if it's OK to play on a local Futsal team (if offered in your area) - Futsal is backed by the USDA and is a staple in many parts of the country now. Playing in a futsal league during your club season may or may not be advisable, depending on your weekly load (the volume of training and games you already have with your club). But, if you only train three times a week, playing on a Futsal team on one of your off days can be beneficial. It doesn't even have to be high level - it could be a pick up team with your friends. This may not stretch you soccer-wise, but it does offer a very beneficial mental recharger.

Girls, ask to train with the boys - I don't think I need to spend much time explaining this. It's pretty well documented that a talented girl playing soccer with boys can be the right amount of stretch and reach to accelerate development. Even if it's once a week.

Ask coach for your "Individual Development Plan (IDP)" - This is not an evaluation. It is a specific developmental map through the next two to five years. Chances are high that your coach or club doesn't have one for you because IDP's are not yet mainstream as standard operating procedure in 2016. It requires a significant tax on a coach's time beyond the obligatory evaluation, but because your appetite for soccer is greater than your fellow teammates and you will likely be the only one making a request like this, it's possible your coach may have the time to do this for you.

Ask coach to make a prediction on your near future - A fair request. Ask your coach to try to look into the future based on his or her experience and offer some possible pathways that they envision for you. This can range from trying a new position, to experimenting with a leadership role, to playing up, etc.. It could even mean a mutually beneficial departure from the club.

Ask coach if you will be allowed to train with a coach outside of the club - We are talking about a Personal Trainer (PT), as discussed earlier. Very few clubs are full service clubs where they provide adequate technical detail and feedback in their training. It's not really the club's fault. Unless it's a residential club, it's just not economical. Policies and reactions to personal training varies greatly from club to club, so it is a good idea to ask about this.

If you are unhappy with your team or situation, ask coach if - a) you are on the right team...and why, or b) if you would be better off with another club. Try to be savvy enough to detect when the coach is just telling you what you want to hear just to keep you (and your fee) in the club. They are tough, straight forward questions to present. But, if you are not happy about your current circumstances, you owe it to yourself to explore your options. It happens every tryout season.

Changing clubs can be difficult. Keep in mind, there is no such thing as a perfect club. Every club has issues. But, there is such a thing as 'a good fit.' Parents, you are your child's biggest advocate, and your job is to do the research and seek the best fit, much like you will do when it's time to help with the college search. For the older players, this is on you. It would be wise to use your network and social media connections to learn about alternatives.

However, as a rule, "When in doubt, stay put."

A word about club-hopping. Beware, because it seems to me that it is getting more and more popular for players to run to another club after the first sign of adversity or disappointment, especially in markets that have multiple Academy teams. History shows that these are the same players who seek a transfer after their first year of college ball, because they haven't learned to fight for their right to play more. Again, this is not across the board, because I have seen some players stuck in bad situations, but by and large I do not condone players running without a fight. As the Beastie Boys sang in their teenage anthem, "You've got to fight…For your right…To party!"

For the older players: **Ask coach (or club rep) about what kind of assistance you can expect in your search for a suitable college** - Some clubs have this piece built into their program, some don't. If your club doesn't offer assistance in this way, start making the connections now. Ask other parents who may have gone through the process with older children. This is a very complex and time consuming process and will require assistance and significant navigation.

Sound advice for parents: Seek a local, experienced, rational person that you trust who is not affiliated with your club, that you feel comfortable with discussing your child's soccer situations. If they are affiliated with a different or rival club, it's a matter of trust. They often have a perspective that you cannot have. You don't have to go this alone. There are people out there who are qualified and willing to help you.

STEP 12

Network

For Parents

Start schmoozing! Networking opens doors. I know parents that have kept a pretty thick catalog of contacts of parents and coaches from different cities and states that they struck up conversations with at such events as 3v3 and various other tournaments, which has led to some amazing out of state guest player experiences for their sons and daughters. These kinds of experiences are good for players who seek "next level" development because it gets them out of their comfort zone and contributes to the development of their personalty, among other things.

Another good reason for networking is to be as aware and as enlightened as you can be regarding the nature and culture of elite soccer in your area.

Don't be afraid to call parents and coaches from other clubs. Discuss and compare experiences. Call your state association with simple questions or concerns. You might be surprised with some of their answers and who they can put you in contact with.

Networking helps you to be that much more aware and is the best protection for you and your child from being misguided or taken advantage of. The hard part is knowing who to trust because so much of modern elite soccer is a business and lines can get blurred pretty easily. Seemingly honorable coaches and club reps spewing company lines just to get your 2K-3K. When in doubt, trust your instincts and go with your gut. Your ability to detect sincerity is key here.

Summary & Final Thoughts

I hope you have enjoyed the ride! It was a blast putting this together for you. There is a lot to digest in this book, and if you reread it you will pick up something new or something that you just plain missed the first time around. It's like watching a movie for the second time in a week. You always notice things that you didn't see when you first saw it.

So...

How will you know if you are successful?

Answer: Making measurable progress in reasonable time. Some things you will need to do daily, like eat right and get proper rest. Other things you can measure in a week, like how many hours did you spend on the ball and do you need another hour on your own to make the goal for the week? Some need a month. Some a year. Some a few years. Everyday you can and should be working toward your dreams, targets and goals.

The pleasure of playing soccer and the discipline of practice are in a constant battle for your attention. It's a kind of dance where the sense of joy justifies the labor, and the labor leads to joy. The discipline in practice is in the striving, and this striving is always colliding with your limits. The constraints of your physical limitations, and your technical limitations and your creative limitations are a burden that you carry daily. Keep moving forward. Embrace the struggle! Keep bumping up against your limitations every day and watch those limitations turn into 'This is too easy!', and then you will be on to the next cycle of learning, with newer and more challenging limitations.

> "Your game does not get better by chance, it gets better by change."

Be proactive.

Change...on purpose.

Live...on purpose.

Train...on purpose.

Play...on purpose.

It all needs to be intentional. Don't leave it to chance.

You are now equipped with a handful of ideas, tools, and resources to help you become the best person and soccer player that you can be.

> "Take good counsel and accept correction - that is the way to live wisely and well."
>
> – King Solomon

I'm going to sign off by leaving you with this quote. It's not from a soccer player, but from a pretty good American sportsmen!

> "You gotta have fun. Regardless of how you look at it, we're playing a game...I don't think you can do well unless you're having fun"
>
> – Derek Jeter, New York Yankees

WORKSHEET #12 - **Comprehensive Box Check** Check all boxes that you are currently doing or working on to get a look at how much you are doing vs. how much you could be doing!

Extra Time!

Some Of My Favorite Soccer Quotes

"In football, the worst blindness is only seeing the ball."
– Nelson Falcão Rodrigues

"The first 90 minutes are the most important."
– Sir Bobby Robson

"Football is all very well as a game for rough girls, but is hardly suitable for delicate boys."
- Oscar Wilde

"I do not play football, I score goals."
– Dario José dos Santos

"If you're in the penalty area and don't know what to do with the ball, put it in the net and we'll discuss the options later."
- Bob Paisley

"**F**ootball is a simple game; 22 men chase a ball for 90 minutes and at the end, the Germans win." – Gary Lineker

"**S**ome people tell me that we professional players are soccer slaves. Well, if this is slavery, give me a life sentence." – Sir Bobby Charlton

"**T**he ball is round, the game lasts ninety minutes, and everything else is just theory." – Josef "Sepp" Herberger

"**I** never thought I'd play soccer past high school, so to go from that team to actually being most-capped and three World Cups is pretty special." – Cobi Jones, US International

"**W**hoever invented soccer should be worshipped as god." – Hugo Sánchez

About The Author

By Dr. Don Grossnickle

Tony Kees has been a prominent fixture in the metro Chicagoland youth soccer community for over 34 years at the writing of this book. He has always been one of the most respected coaches on every platform of the youth game, and not just for his soccer acumen, which is at the highest level, but for his intense study of the game and appreciation for the science of soccer as well as the aesthetics of the game! Tony has been a thought leader, visionary, change agent and mentor to so many and has always been regarded as one of the busiest coaches in Chicago. I remember a stretch of years where he juggled the Academy, ODP, high school and managed his own club (EG Arsenal). Among his many strengths, though, and by far his best attribute is the depth of caring, understanding and compassion for the players in front of him, as well as that rare ability to connect with players at every age. If you watch him work, you can see his 'connection before content' approach. Underpinning all of this, of course is his background in education. Once upon a time TK was an art teacher, and a good one. He understands how children learn and has brought that out to the field with him. His creative nature has always made things fun, challenging and interesting for his players!

Besides Tony's team coaching, he has worked individually with many of Illinois' top players in personal settings, gaining valuable experience in working with the mind of elite athletes. In recent years, he has been involved in a side project where he is Co-owner of Step Ahead Sports Soccer Center Of Excellence, specializing in Futsal and Sports Performance (SAQ and Technical Training). This human performance laboratory has given him a high tech home for his over-the-top performance training.

When asked what has driven his professional coaching career, Tony simply says, "I think I'm just naturally curious. I am always thinking that there is a better way. The status quo is not my friend!"

When asked what gets him out of bed every morning: "Two things: 1) to put myself squarely in the asset column of life every day, and 2) to make a difference in someone's life."

This book has that written all over it!

SERVICE 2016 (short list)

• Chicago Fire, Assistant Academy Director & Staff Coach (5 yrs)

• Chicago Fire, Academy Staff Coach (Sports Performance) (2 yrs)

• Chicago Magic-PSG, Academy Staff Coach (1 yr)

• Chicago Inferno, PDL Head Coach (1 yr)

• EG Arsenal Club, DOC (22 yrs)

• Illinois ODP (25 yrs)

• James B. Conant HS, Head Boys Coach (21 yrs)

• Neuqua Valley HS Head Boys Coach (3 yrs)

• Elk Grove HS, Head Girls Coach, (3 yrs)

ACCOLADES

- National Champions, Chicago Fire Academy U16 2010

- National Champions, IL ODP '89 Boys

- National Champions, IL ODP '90 Boys

- National Champions, IL ODP '91 Boys

- I.H.S.S.C.A (High School) Coach of the Year 2007

- I.Y.S.A (Club) Competitive Coach of the Year 2007

CERTIFICATION

USSF 'A' License

NSCAA Premier Diploma

KNVB Advanced Match Analysis Certificate

LaLiga Formation Methodology Level 3 Certificate

US Youth Futsal Level 4 Certification

EDUCATION

Bachelor of Science in Education (Art), Northern Arizona University '82

PLAYING CAREER

Though never signing a pro contract, Tony kicked around in the pro indoor circuit with the Kansas City Comets and Illinois Thunder

INTERESTS

Making sports paintings, inventing board games, playing guitar